Tour de Faith

A CYCLIST'S LESSONS FOR LIVING

ROBERT
MOLSBERRY

COWLEY PUBLICATIONS
Lanham, Chicago, New York, Toronto, and Plymouth, UK

Published by Cowley Publications
An imprint of Rowman & Littlefield Publishers, Inc.
A wholly owned subsidiary of The Rowman & Littlefield Publishing Group, Inc.
4501 Forbes Boulevard, Suite 200
Lanham, MD 20706

Estover Road
Plymouth PL6 7PY
United Kingdom

Distributed by National Book Network

Library of Congress Cataloging-in-Publication Data

Molsberry, Robert F.
Tour de faith : a cyclist's lessons for living / Robert Molsberry.
p. cm.
ISBN-13: 978-1-56101-316-6 (pbk. : alk. paper)
ISBN-10: 1-56101-316-1 (pbk. : alk. paper)
1. Christian life. 2. Cycling. 3. RAGBRAI (Bicycle race).
4. Bicycle racing. I. Title.
BV4501.3.M646 2007
242—dc22 2007008479

Printed in the United States of America.

♾™ The paper used in this publication meets the minimum requirements of American National Standard for Information Sciences—Permanence of Paper for Printed Library Materials, ANSI/NISO Z39.48-1992.

John Thomas

Tour de Faith

Contents

INTRODUCTION

Making Meaning Out of a Bike Ride Across Iowa

YOU CAN learn a great deal about life from the seat of a bicycle as you pedal across the state of Iowa summer after summer. You'll learn, for example, that the value of life is in the journey, not the destination. You'll learn that it sometimes takes a whole community of friends and strangers to get you where you need to be. Try to go it alone and you'll find yourself in trouble. So take care of your friends along the way. You'll learn that life is a celebration, even when suffering and death are occasional companions. And, by the second or third day of the ride, you'll learn perhaps the most practical lesson of the week: which saddle sore cream works best on your butt.

Every summer, rain or shine, gainfully employed or "between things," with or without my family, with my wife's blessing or not, fit or flabby, I participate in the *Des Moines Register*'s Annual Great Bicycle Ride Across Iowa (better known around the Midwest as RAGBRAI). It's a bike ride like no other, in terms of size, length, and history: four or five hundred miles in seven days of riding, from the Missouri River on the western edge of Iowa to the Mississippi River on the east; ten thousand participants riding their bikes from one little Iowa town to another, day after day for a week, with several thousand groupies along to drive support vehicles, sell things to the riders, or just join them for parties every night. RAGBRAI has a thirty-five-year history, with no end in sight.

But this isn't a book about a bike ride. This is a book about life; about what you can learn about life by riding your bike four or five hundred miles across Iowa every summer. Every day on the road, funny and touching and intriguing things happen. Every night the riders gather around coolers full of beer and Gatorade and soda in town parks and county fairgrounds to share their stories. The stories grow larger with each telling, and meaning is made in the process. Every time I ride RAGBRAI, I listen to the stories and gather them up along with my own. I discern what larger meanings might reverberate from the stories, and then I package them as a sermon to present to my congregation. I'm a United Church of Christ pastor, you see, and I'll stoop to any low to get sermon ideas.

It's always RAGBRAI Sunday in my church the day after the ride is over. I've had as many as twenty or thirty riders show up for worship that day, wearing their biking jerseys and spandex shorts, to hear what I have to say about them and, in some cases, to defend themselves. There's always a distinctive odor in the sanctuary on that Sunday. Not every cyclist in attendance has had time to rinse out his or her jersey and shorts from the previous day's ride. We encourage riders to bring their bikes right into the sanctuary, so the decorating committee arranges bikes rather than flowers that day. Sometimes my regular congregation comes, too, although I suspect that many of my members use RAGBRAI Sunday as an excuse to sleep in or visit the Methodist church down the block. No matter. Church is always full and it's always a good time, swapping yarns and tall tales about the ride. As you might imagine, the stories get grander with each telling. In fact, some of the stories in this book have been told and retold so many times they now bear only a casual resemblance to what might have actually happened. In that, they resemble the controversial question of the factual historicity of biblical stories. But, also like the question of biblical truth, the factual literal truth of some of these RAGBRAI claims is less relevant than the fact that they *should* be true, whether they actually happened or not. Truth should never be limited to narrowly observable historical fact.

This book is a collection of some of the best lessons for living that I've gleaned from my RAGBRAI rides over the years. They're not all original ideas, I'm afraid. Besides my own experiences and those I've overheard around ice chest conversations at the end of a day's ride, I've often asked the charter group I ride with to share their experiences with me. Sometimes, on the bus ride out to the western edge of the state, I give them an assignment. "Collect stories for me from your week of riding that illustrate the meaning of life." I keep it pretty general. And then I'll hop on the bus at the end of the ride and ask if any stories have been gathered. I feel like a fisherman casting a net in the sea. I never know what I'll reel in. Some riders have actually kept notes. And then, one story leads to another and plenty of material gets generated. But I've tried, at least, to give credit where credit is due.

My wife, Ann (bless her heart) pointed out to me, after these reflections were written down, that some of them seem to contradict each other. In one chapter, for example, I quote Catholic theologian Matthew Fox in claiming that life is not a problem to be solved, but a mystery that is bigger than ourselves and therefore ultimately unsolvable. You simply have to stand in awe at the sight of it, mouth hanging open in appreciation. But then in another chapter I quote Scott Peck, author of *The Road Less Traveled*, who defines life precisely as a set of problems to be solved, implying that a perfectly disciplined individual could solve all problems.

This created something of a dilemma for me.

But wait, Ann said (what a dear!), there's more. You talk at one point about the need to get our work done, to climb those hills, in order to receive our reward of cold watermelon and Gatorade. But then you also talk about being attentive to the moment, no matter how difficult it may be, and finding enjoyment in the here-and-now.

She was right (darn her), absolutely right. I checked the chapters in question and found discrepancies. I knew that tightly knit theological systems could not stand with internal contradictions. They would crumble like a house of cards. I would have to dismantle my whole opus and try to reconstruct it.

But then I was saved by the realization that I was not constructing a tightly-knit, logically consistent, internally coherent theological system. I was simply reflecting on a bike ride, a most disorganized, illogical undertaking. All of life is a contradiction. If you try to reconcile every aspect of life, you'll just drive yourself crazy. Even Qoheleth, the author of the Wisdom book of Ecclesiastes in the Old Testament, understands the contradictory nature of life.

> For everything there is a season, and a time for every
> matter under heaven:
> A time to be born, and a time to die;
> A time to plant, and a time to pluck up what is planted;
> A time to kill, and a time to heal;
> A time to break down, and a time to build up;
> A time to weep, and a time to laugh;
> A time to mourn, and a time to dance. (Ecclesiastes 3:1-4)

I often say that every sermon is a heresy. Its opposite is equally as true. I could preach a sermon one week on Paul's affirmation that we are saved only by faith, not by works. Paul says all we have to do is believe and trust. We don't have to prove our worth by doing good deeds; good deeds aren't going to get us into heaven.

But then the following week, or to a different congregation, I could just as easily preach on James, who says that faith without works is dead. "Show me your faith apart from your works, and I by my works will show you my faith" (James 2:18). James commands the faithful to be doers of the word, not just hearers. Each of these two apparently contradictory messages is equally true. One group of listeners might need to hear the message of faith as trust. Another group might need to be told to get up off their duffs and do something productive to live out their beliefs. Or the same group might need to hear both messages, but at different times. I've found that it's the same for almost every Great Biblical Truth. The opposite of every Great Biblical Truth could be preached with equal legitimacy. Which leads me to the conclusion that there are no Great Truths, only firmly held human interpretations of the truth. Paul says we see reality in a mirror, dimly (1 Corinthians 13:12). Nobody is in sole possession of the Truth in its entirety (if such a thing even exists). Which further leads me to wonder why so many of us are so entrenched in our own versions of the truth that we are willing to lynch, assassinate, and drop smart bombs on those who hold to other versions. People, come on. We're only defending personal perspectives. Can't we all just get along?

So my RAGBRAI reflections might seem to be contradictory. Okay, so shoot me. But as they bump up against one another, perhaps creative thinking will occur in the tension. Maybe one reflection will resonate with you, but its alternative may cause you to stop and think. I make no attempt to force any of these thoughts into a coherent, logical system. That would be a shame, a violation of the RAGBRAI spirit. I let the experiences along the road speak for themselves. RAGBRAI, like life, is a rolling contradiction. Maybe that's my first lesson.

Crossing Iowa is a metaphor. It conjures up other crossings. The Hebrews in the book of Exodus crossed the Jordan River on their way toward inheriting a land flowing with milk and honey. But crossing the Jordan signified an arrival for them. The people of Israel had been wandering in the wilderness for forty years, all the while hoping and praying for this moment of termination. Crossing the Jordan meant the journey was over. God's promises had been fulfilled. Crossing Iowa is a completely different sort of adventure, as we'll see in the second chapter. Crossing Iowa by bicycle is not about getting anywhere in particular. The value, in the case of RAGBRAI, is not in the arrival, but in the meandering. Actually, if the Hebrew people had been really attentive to what was going on, they would have realized that it was the formative nature of their journey in the wilderness, rather than in the inheritance of a promised land, that was to have the greater impact on their life as a people. It was in the wilderness that they came together as a community; it was in the wilderness that they received the Ten Commandments, which identified them as the people of the Torah ("law"); and it was in the wilderness that their relationship with their God was formed.

How does meaning bubble up out of the experience of pedaling one's bicycle across Iowa? Raw experience happens, but, without some interpretation, it remains meaningless. I think you can go through life without ever reflecting on your experience or learning anything from it. In fact, I know some people who pride themselves in not learning anything along the way. They're called fundamentalists. Many even hold high political office.

Socrates said, "The unexamined life is not worth living." But many people do, in fact, lead unexamined lives. They don't think, they don't cross-examine their experiences and philosophies, they fall easy prey to those selling the snake oil of absolute certainty. And maybe the unexamined certainties they swallow help them get by with whatever difficulties they may be facing at the moment. But they may be missing the abundant joy of life lived out beyond the safe and secure and comfortable.

A little reflection will organize raw experience into patterns that begin to exhibit meaning. I discovered this when I was living in Managua, working with the Mennonite Central Committee from 1991 through 1994. I taught community development to local Mennonite church leaders. It was very interesting. The days were full of unique experiences. I was engaged and active, always busy in lively, exotic circumstances as I visited rural communities and taught my workshops. But what did the experiences mean?

They didn't mean much of anything until I started writing little articles for publication back in the States. I'd write about the devastating effects of U.S. backed neoliberal policies on the lives of ordinary people in Nicaragua. And I would illustrate these claims with stories that I would witness on the street or encounters I would have out in the countryside. The little boy who offered to "watch" my truck for a small fee, for example (a budding capitalist, learning the fine art of extortion), the family digging a hole for a latrine on a vacant lot where they were planning a squatters' settlement—they all told stories that became a biting critique of U.S. foreign policy when they were gathered up along with data and reflection. Once I saw the circumstances around me through the prism of global politics and economics, they started to mean something.

In the same way, RAGBRAI experience is just a fun pastime until you put a spin of meaning on it. There's nothing wrong with having a fun pastime every summer. Lord knows we need all the fun we can get in this life. But when you can have fun and still be theologically reflective about things, that's the mother lode. Then real life lessons begin to emerge. That's what I do. I do theological reflection on daily experience. That's why they pay me the big bucks.

I make no apology for the ruminations that bubble up in response to my experiences on the road. Initially I was worried about offending some of my readers with my political, ecclesiastical, or social slant on things. Surely I've butchered someone's sacred cow here. In fact, given the way the general population has evenly divided into red states and blue states during recent elections, I suspect my reflections may offend about 50 percent of the population. But they're my reflections, they come from the heart, and I accept any fallout that might result. If they challenge your heartfelt convictions, let's sit down over coffee and hash things out. Or, better yet, let's get on our bikes and ride a few miles together and see what emerges.

Actually, that strategy has served me well in the past. A beloved former church member and I used to ride and race and swim together all the time. We spent hours out on the roads and in the swimming pool together, challenging each other to ever greater feats of endurance and strength. Over the years it turned out that we had almost nothing else in common. He was a staunch Republican; I'm a flaming liberal. He believed in saving; I believe in spending. He would hold fund-raising events for political candidates who I regarded as barbaric. I would post notices about liberal causes on the church bulletin board and he would want to know when his church had become the headquarters of the Democratic Party in our county. But he hung in there, bless his heart, because we had one thing in common: we had shared much sweat and many miles. We had a relationship.

Jesus calls us to relationship, not agreement on doctrine.

That's what I value about my denomination, the United Church of Christ. We can differ on issues of substance, but we can still sit down together at the table of grace. One of our predecessor denominations brought over from Germany the covenant, "In essentials, unity. In nonessentials, diversity. In all things, charity." This is a uniquely valuable bumper-sticker in today's world of increasing polarization. A new slogan that describes our denomination says, "No matter who you are or where you are on life's journey, you're welcome here." Of course, that's the very value that gets us in trouble with fundamentalists, who would never dream of ever sitting down with anyone who disagreed with them.

I wonder if that same strategy might work with the Bush administration and Al-Qaeda. What would happen if George W. and Osama were forced to ride together for the week of RAGBRAI, to share a pup tent and watermelon and porta-potties? Would there be greater mutual understanding? Would Mr. Bin Laden develop a greater appreciation for Western ways? Or would he, on the basis of reputed RAGBRAI excesses observable during the week, find himself reconfirmed in his opinion that we're all a bunch of hedonists over here? Would Mr. Bush come to understand the seething anger of Muslim extremists who feel the weight of centuries of oppression at the hands of the West? During the week of RAGBRAI, at least, there would be no planning of terrorist plots or bombing raids. At the end of a RAGBRAI day there would be little energy or inclination left over to plan acts of war. Call this my modest proposal for world peace.

In spite of the haphazard nature of my reflections on the RAGBRAI bicycle ride and the apparent contradictions that surface, a remarkably coherent set of affirmations about life emerges. I call it my manifesto on life. Taken as a whole, these affirmations place me squarely in the Progressive Christian camp, a loose but growing movement of liberal voices clamoring for attention today. This book might even be considered a Progressive Christian primer, with spokes and wheels, an introduction for the novice to a whole new way of looking at the faith. It will become clear that my theology has little in common with the theology of the conservative, evangelical, fundamentalist wing of Christianity, the wing that is usually cited these days when media commentators refer to "Christian voters" or the "religious influence on politics." Although I consider myself a deeply religious person, and I live out my faith in the social and political arena, my views never seem to be at the table when the media is talking about morals or values or faith in politics. My Christian convictions about the death penalty, war, poverty, access to health care and employment, freedom of choice, and civil rights for gays and lesbians are never mentioned when "moral issues" are discussed. It's as if there are two completely different Christianities in operation here, and mine is never represented. Why is that? How have the conservatives co-opted the discussion?

This progressive strand of Christianity is just now reemerging and finding its voice. I say "reemerging" because it has previously played a major role in American history. Progressive faith has not always been as invisible or marginalized as it has become during the last couple of presidential elections.

> Movements in American history fueled by the energy of religious progressives include the Abolitionist Movement, Women's Suffrage, the Social Gospel Movement, Conscientious Objection to War, Trade Unions, the New Deal, Civil Rights, opposition to the Vietnam and Iraq Wars,

> the elimination of racism, and many aspects of contemporary feminism including reproductive rights, marriage freedom, equality for gays and lesbians, and the inclusion of sexual minorities.[1]

Progressive, prophetic faith has often taken a front seat on peace and justice issues, calling for a compassionate society that more closely resembled the world Jesus advocated. It's just been silent here lately.

Well, let it be mute no longer. In my book it emerges from the adventures on an annual bicycle romp across the state of Iowa.

As you read the various lessons that surface from my reflections on RAGBRAI you may discern the following three affirmations woven throughout. First and foremost, I affirm that life is good. In spite of the Iowa humidity and temperatures that can combine to produce heat indices of 110, 120 degrees, life is good. In spite of hills and headwinds, long miles, rain and storms, life is good. In spite of crippling accidents and even death, life is good. If we didn't believe that, we wouldn't be on RAGBRAI. The biblical model we embrace is God's action in placing humankind in a generous garden, ripe with all we would need to enjoy life. Before there was original sin and punishment, there was original blessing.[2] Before anything else and above all, we are blessed. The contemporary version of this garden is Iowa in the last full week in July, when the corn is growing so fast you can almost see it and ten thousand loony bicyclists are having the time of their lives out on the rural highways. RAGBRAI is fun. Did I mention that yet? Families are bonding, bodies are getting fit, a compassionate community is constructed, even if only for a week, and local towns and villages are challenged to work together like never before to provide hospitality.

Life is good. The worst day on RAGBRAI is better than the best day at work, I always say. We know that bad things will happen, but living in the confidence that we are surrounded by people who love and care for us and in the certainty of God's gracious presence, we live in hope that whatever happens will be okay. To put it in the vernacular, the glass is half full. There is a silver lining to every cloud. There's a light at the end of the tunnel. The sun will come out tomorrow, bet your bottom dollar. It's a good world we live in.

A second affirmation builds on the first. You couldn't have the second without the first, in fact. The second affirmation is that life is a journey of exploration and adventure, not a safe and secure landing place. We're not, in this life, in some cosmic holding pattern. We're on a pilgrimage. If RAGBRAI is any indicator, that should be obvious. People who participate in RAGBRAI don't do it to arrive somewhere; they do it to enjoy the road and all it has to offer. The great treat on the route is the myriad offerings of food, hospitality, and entertainment that pop up along the side of the road and at the tops of hills and in small town squares mile after mile. It's the relationships that form and playful ways they are acted out during the week. Every day brings something new. It takes a great spirit of adventure to continue on the ride during days of harsh conditions. Not everyone is up to the challenge. But for those with an explorer's heart, the rewards are great.

The journey of RAGBRAI is not for everyone. Lodging, riding conditions, the availability of food—they're all uncertain from day to day. Many people need things settled and nailed down. They lament that so much of modern life is in flux that they need the security of certainty in some areas of their lives. They are threatened by change and diversity, and would never in a million years take a real journey of discovery on which they might run the risk of being transformed. They're the ones with bumper stickers that read, "God said it; I believe it; that settles it." A sad lot, they are, but, sadly, powerful. They seek to pass legislation defining who is okay and who isn't, setting boundaries between the acceptable and unacceptable, building fences, defending their version of the truth against all who would threaten it. Religion for them is a defense of righteousness. I say this group is a sad lot, because they'll never be open to whatever new things life might have in store for them.

To me, life is a great adventure, a gift that we open up fresh every morning. It's like Christmas morning every day. If you hunker down where you are, circle the wagons, and conclude you've already seen it all, I believe you've rejected the gift and turned your back on the giver. A pity.

A third affirmation picks up the first two. Along the way on this journey through a good and nurturing world, we're supposed to be nice to one another. That, to me, is the heart of the gospel, the point of life, and the meaning of everything. That's what the Bible comes to in the end, the whole of the Christian ethic in a nutshell. On RAGBRAI when you're out there on the road, you take care of one another. You stop for riders in trouble. You share food. You arrive together, building one another up along the way.

The heart of the gospel is not proper beliefs or legislated behavior. It is not about judgment. The gospel is not about doctrines and dogma. It's not about adhering to a specified set of principles. It certainly isn't a resource to justify warfare against people who don't believe the same things we do. How could we have gotten it so absolutely wrong? The Bible at its core summons people into community, providing an alternative vision of a compassionate world in which all people are treated fairly. The vision seems radical to us because our world doesn't reflect these values. We're into competition, power, wealth, status, and war. The Bible promotes compassion, hospitality, generosity, and justice. These are two very different systems for ordering human relations.

On RAGBRAI, for a week every summer, people begin to dabble in that second vision, God's vision, in ways they never get to during the rest of the year. People take care of one another. Stronger riders push weaker riders up the hills. Families open their homes to complete strangers so they can take a shower and get rested. Farmers haul exhausted cyclists into town. Lions lie down with lambs. Well, that's an exaggeration. But I did see buffalos, llamas, cows, and ostriches in a field together one time. Does that count?

So, on RAGBRAI we learn the basics. Life is good. Our time here on earth is a journey of discovery and joy. And the journey is best traveled in the company of others who travel with us. All the rest, including the relative effectiveness of various antichaffing creams, is just details. Although I highly recommend Desitin ointment.

As I wrap up the writing of this book, it occurs to me that I may be setting up many of my readers for disappointment. Some of you picked up this book because you're into bicycling. Others found it because you're students of progressive Christian theology. Those of you who are students of theology may be impatient with all this talk about bicycling. "Who cares about RAGBRAI," you might be muttering under your breath. "Get on with the theology." But those of you who are cyclists may be just as impatient with the theological sections of the book. I can just hear you complaining, "Enough of this church stuff. Let's get back to the bike ride." I can sympathize with both, but they present something of a dilemma.

I have two possible solutions for you both. My first suggestion is that you just skip the pages you don't like. Cyclists, you won't have to plow through more than four or five pages of theological reflection before you find another satisfying bicycle adventure. Theological seekers, you may have to put up with a few more pages of bicycling, but don't fret. There's more theological reflection to come. You both may want to just rip out the offending sections in each chapter. That will lighten the total weight of the book and make it easier for you to stick it in your camping gear (for you cyclists) or your brief cases (for you theologians). You might even approach the publisher to get half your money back from the purchase of the book. If only half the book appeals to you, why should you have to pay for the whole thing? I'm not guaranteeing that they'll actually give you the refund, but it never hurts to ask.

My other suggestion is to be patient. Read the whole darn thing, even the boring sections that don't appeal to you. You might just learn something.

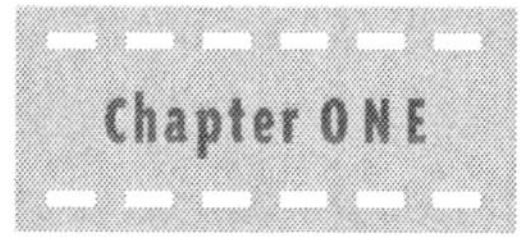

The Best Bike Ride on the Planet

IT'S SIX O'CLOCK in the morning and the mist is still in the valleys, hugging wooded creek beds. We're bicycling smoothly along rural highways through cornfields and stands of trees that are highlighted in a red-orange horizontal light from the sun, just peeking over the horizon. Shadows are long as the road undulates over gentle rises and disappears into the distance. Before the sun is overhead and turns the whole scene into a sweltering blast furnace, Iowa is a lush green garden. Grant Wood painted these scenes. Once you've seen them yourself, you'll realize that he painted them true to form, only very slightly idealized.

The breeze is cool on our faces, and spirits are high. I'm surrounded by ten thousand other riders enjoying the same vistas, and we're sharing stories of yesterday's ride or last night's adventures as we spin easily to loosen up sore muscles. It's going to be a good day. They're all good days, someone behind us points out. This is RAGBRAI, and life doesn't get any better.

Even if you're not a big bicycling fanatic like I am, you've got to be impressed with the RAGBRAI phenomenon. RAGBRAI is an organized (I use the term loosely) seven-day bicycle tour across Iowa that takes place the last full week in July every summer. On average, ten thousand cyclists participate, with another several thousand showing up for the party. The name RAGBRAI, in case you were wondering, is an acronym that stands for the *Des Moines Register*'s Annual Great Bicycle Ride

Across Iowa. The organizers are even now, as I write this, hard at work planning the next edition of the ride. They may, for all I know, already have the one after that in the can.

It began in 1973 as a clever scheme by two reporters with the *Des Moines Register* to get the newspaper to pay them to take a week off to ride their bikes across the state. It was the beginning of the bicycling craze (pre-spandex), John Karras and Donald Kaul liked cycling, and they wanted to see Iowa. They figured that if they wrote daily columns about the ride, they could claim to be working and thus eligible for pay. They invited readers to join them and were flummoxed when three hundred people actually showed up. I watched that rag-tag outfit roll through Iowa City, just one week before I was off to start my freshman year at college. There were no arrangements made for the three hundred cyclists to cross the state; the towns they would be passing through had not been warned; little in the way of lodging or food had been prepared in advance. But they had so much fun and they generated so much interest across the state, they did it again the next year. This time, a couple thousand riders appeared.

I was one of them.

Back then we were all a bunch of young, scraggly, long-haired hippie-types, wearing cut-offs and tee shirts and sneakers. I used to cut my hair once a year, whether it needed it or not. Helmets were for sissies, except for one eight-three-year-old gentleman by the name of Clarence Pickard who wore an authentic British pith helmet. The adjectives "young," "scraggly," "long-haired," and "hippie-type" also did not apply to him. He swore by long pants and shirt sleeves, with woolen long johns and a wool sweater underneath. He said they insulated him from the heat of the sun. He became an instant celebrity, epitomizing the spirit of the ride. The ride was so unique in 1974 that people in small towns and farms along the route came out and gave us food and drink for free all week. We all felt like celebrities, which, in a way, we were.

But those days are gone. Today RAGBRAI is big business. John Karras, in his exhaustive history of the ride, says, "What began as a modest lark has turned into an industry."[3] Now the *Des Moines Register* has a whole office dedicated to the organization and implementation of RAGBRAI. It's full time for three paid staff members year round, but their numbers swell with additional hired and volunteer staff as the date of the ride approaches. What started as a free romp across the state now costs $125 for participants to register (the cost covers the liability insurance and ride support provided by the *Des Moines Register*). And then you have to figure in the cost of a private bus charter to the start of the ride and back home after it's over, the equipment you're riding on and carrying, and the cost of food. Plan on spending six to eight bucks for a meal, and eating about six times a day to keep the body fueled. And then there's the beer. I don't recommend skimping on beer when you're out in the sun exercising all day every day. You have to keep up your strength. RAGBRAI is no longer a cheap jaunt. But to my mind, it's worth every penny.

Coming into its thirty-fifth year, RAGBRAI riders coming through a town can put an enterprising Boy Scout troop or a struggling church or a playground organization in the black: fifteen thousand riders and support crew members each drop up to $20 per night for food and entertainment in the tiny towns that host them, and that money goes to the chicken-grilling Boy Scouts, the ice-cream scooping church committee, and other local causes. The rolling community that descends upon these small towns sometimes overwhelms the local population by a factor of five or ten to one. The smallest town ever to host overnight was Fayette, population nine hundred. That's fifteen to one. It's only a slight exaggeration to say that the local residents were so intimidated by the approaching sweaty hordes that half of them boarded up their homes and fled. It was something of a challenge even scavenging food that night. One town, early on, posted a sign on the edge of town that read, "Be kind. You outnumber us two to one."

On the other hand, it's not as much fun rolling into some of Iowa's larger towns for the night. Yes, it might surprise you to know, Iowa has cities. We don't all own tractors and live on farms. We have stoplights and parking meters. A few, at least. (In my first parish in a small town in Iowa, I could honestly give directions to the parsonage by saying, "Just go to the only stoplight in the county and turn right.") In a place like Des Moines or Waterloo or Cedar Rapids, even fifteen thousand bike riders can get swallowed up pretty easily. It's as though bigger cities have other things going on—more important things. They don't have time to pay attention to you as you complete the day's ride. They don't care that you overcame the odds and the miles and the heat and the hills and the headwinds to arrive at last at their town. They don't honor the conquering heroes. They have to get their kids to soccer practice. In the small towns, the sheer number of bicyclists can easily shut things down. Literally. You just try to drive around your town when the streets are clogged with hundreds of support vehicles and thousands of bicycles. RAGBRAI becomes the only show in town.

The riders have aged, too. We're not radical, shaggy kids anymore. The average age today is in the mid-forties, as the last of the baby boomers experience a second (or third or fourth) childhood out on the open roads (and in the bars). We tend to be professionals, doctors and lawyers and pastors and business executives. It's not unusual for a cyclist to fall down in a crash and find himself attended by an EMT, a pastor, a brain surgeon, and a trial lawyer who just happened to be pedaling by at the time. The average income level of riders is around $80,000 with 40 percent of riders earning over $100,000 annually.[4]

What's it like spending a week bicycling with ten thousand of your closest friends? I'll do my best to describe a typical day. As though there were typical days on this carnival ride. Most riders camp in city parks or lawns in the overnight town. Colorful mushroom fields of tents start popping up until most every square inch of unclaimed grass in town is covered by tents. As dawn breaks around 5 a.m., the sounds of Velcro ripping open and zippers unzipping are heard. Early morning, before dawn, is the only quiet moment on the whole of the week's ride. It's almost magical as the mist begins to lift from the tenting grounds.

And then they arise. Dopey campers stagger to the nearest porta-potty like a scene from *Night of the Living Dead.* Tents are rolled up and gear stowed. Most of the riders use private charter services now, which provide bus transportation to the western edge of the state for the start of the ride and pick up riders at the eastern terminus at the end of the week. And then, during the week, the charters provide rented trucks or old school buses with volunteer crews who stake out camping territory where their groups settle for the night. So, first thing in the morning, the gear is thrown on the back of the truck and by 6 a.m. the only sign of last night's city of tents is trampled grass. In later years I've begun staying in private homes that graciously open up and let riders crash in spare bedrooms or on the floor. I'll stay in motels where there are vacancies. I even stay in nursing homes when they can locate an extra bed. I'm not proud. The nursing homes are a bit of a challenge, though. Those mild-mannered residents tend to get wild and crazy late at night. Who'd have thought? I try to ride hard enough during the day that I'll really need my rest at night, so I've been leery of relying on conditions in the campground. There have been nights on RAGBRAI during which the temperatures haven't dipped below 95. There's no way I could lie awake sweating all night and then ride again in the morning. Some people do it. My hat's off to them.

Arranging local housing in family homes is an adventure in trust. The first time I did this I sent out letters on my church stationery to local chambers of commerce in the overnight towns, polite letters, respectful. My letters were successful, but my stays that week were with sweet little old ladies and pastors' families.

I wasn't going to do that again.

The next year I wrote funny, crude letters. I promised that me and my posse would try to leave the town's daughters alone and we wouldn't fart in public or spit on the floors unless it proved absolutely necessary. But I seemed to have swung to the other extreme with that letter. That year our lodgings were again problematic, but for entirely different reasons. One of our host families proudly pointed out their custom-made light switches, crafted to resemble a piece of the male anatomy. They had six kegs of beer reserved for my group of four riders, not realizing from my letter that we actually went to bed at nine. We were unmasked as fakes. Our hosts had to go out to the campground to rustle up some authentic party animals.

But it is enjoyable staying with local families. They're genuinely interested in you and your ride. They tend to be pleasant, hospitable people, and they enjoy strolling downtown with their riders and getting into the swing of the party.

Back to the early morning departure scene. It's eerie the way the towns empty out by six a.m. Once I had to be dropped off in one of these overnight towns to start my RAGBRAI ride late. I didn't arrive until 8 a.m. At that hour the local townspeople were not yet up—it had been a late night for them what with all the feeding and hosting and then the partying until the wee hours—and all the bike riders had fled already. Where was everyone, I wanted to know. Had they all been raptured, and I was among the left-behind? At least RAGBRAI is a clean and tidy conquering army. It has often been observed that fields where the hordes have camped are left neater than before they arrived. It's generally a well-behaved, polite mob. Even the late-night crowds fueled by excesses of beer are, with a few notable (and well reported) exceptions, respectful. Exuberant, yes, but rarely mean.

The bike ride begins slowly each morning, with cyclists filling the streets from curb to curb. There's no hurry yet. It will get sunny soon, the crowds will thin out, the heat will rise, and bodies will get into rhythm. But the cool of the morning is delicious, to be savored.

Ten miles down the road you'll find a fire department selling pancakes or breakfast burritos and you can stop for the day's first food. Lines are long at these first stops, but there are always lines on RAGBRAI. There are lines for food, lines for bathrooms, lines for water, lines for air for your bike tires. Usually the best thing to do when you see a line is get in it. Doesn't matter what it's for. It's better to get lined up and be surprised at what you find than to discover later that you needed whatever it was and only then start to queue up. In fact, one rider once claimed that a significant part of her RAGBRAI training consisted of waiting outside her bathroom door every morning for thirty-seven minutes just to get used to the delay.

The average day's ride is sixty to seventy miles. A hardcore cyclist can finish that distance in three hours or less, but most of the riders, wisely, take most of the day, stopping at food stands and entertainment venues provided by the little towns that pop up every ten miles or so. Towns are plentiful in Iowa, not like in Montana or South Dakota. Iowa, you might recall, was settled by pioneers who could travel ten miles or so by wagon in a day, so towns were strategically planted close together. There are ninety-nine counties in Iowa, each county a little square on the map, each county seat (the town where the courthouse is located) placed deliberately at the center of the square for easy access by rural residents who had to get there and back home before dark. Iowa was an orderly place when it was settled.

The riding, for me, is the heart of the experience. I genuinely enjoy rolling along rural highways propelled by my own power. I have always enjoyed cycle touring and have even led church youth groups on cycling excursions. There's camaraderie on the road with RAGBRAI, as the riders all have this experience in common. There are no strangers. It's fun watching the crops and the hills and the little towns roll by. I am calmed by the rhythmic cranking of the pedals.

Personal hygiene on RAGBRAI can be daunting to a novice. Showers are often local car washes. Most towns run completely out of hot water by late afternoon. Sometimes an enterprising entrepreneur will put up hoses and plastic sheeting for walls out in a field by the campsite and sell shower tickets. These makeshift showers are open to the air, so ultralight planes and gliders often hover overhead for a glimpse of nakedness. Nobody cares much. A couple of years ago my grown son, Ames, just started going door to door with a towel and a bar of soap, offering a couple of bucks to anyone kind enough to let him in to take a shower. He never had to knock on more than two or three doors before he got an invitation.

Going to the bathroom is also a learned response on RAGBRAI. Along the route, most cyclists just veer off into a roadside cornfield when they feel the call of nature. Some local farmers make a gag of it by placing rolls of toilet paper on top of fence posts along their fields. I heard a story once about a city fellow who had a little difficulty with our earthy Iowa solutions. It seems he asked a more seasoned cyclist what to do about relieving himself along the route. The advice given was to simply step a few yards into a cornfield and do your business. Corn grows seven or eight feet tall, you see, and provides complete privacy. Some time later the seasoned advice-giver was surprised to see his new friend peeing in plain sight in the middle of a soybean field. Soybeans only grow a couple of feet tall. The poor city slicker didn't know the difference between the two crops.

Which brings me to another aspect of the ride: Iowa's diverse scenery. Most people, when they think of Iowa, think of a flat wasteland planted in a monocrop of corn. Well, nothing could be further from the truth. They must be mistaking Iowa with Nebraska or Kansas. Iowa has gently rolling hills, and a few stands of trees here and there. And the agricultural diversity is stunning. For a few miles you're rolling along with corn on your right and soybeans on your left, and then all of a sudden, everything changes and it's like you're in a whole different world—now there are soybeans on your right and corn on the other side. Sometimes there's corn on both sides.

Rolling along at fifteen or sixteen miles an hour when conditions are perfect is very close to heaven, in my mind. When it's cool (cool is a relative term on RAGBRAI; at this time of year in Iowa, cool is anything under 95 degrees with a humidity reading under 100 percent), and the road is flat and the wind not in your face, RAGBRAI can generate an almost spiritual sense of well-being. Once I was riding in such conditions with my daughter, who was just eight or nine at the time. It was relatively quiet on the road on a beautiful morning, when a stranger's voice broke the reverie. "Uh oh," he said from somewhere behind us, "I'm feeling bubbly!" I was beginning to worry over what he might have meant, when he breezed past us followed by a swarm of bubbles he'd been blowing from one of those little bubble wands in the plastic bottles. The bubbles danced and soared behind him, reflecting the sun and bouncing off the riders all around us. It was almost a holy moment, so beautiful and funny and surprising that we almost had to stop to appreciate it.

But then there are bad days, too. Way back in the 1980s, when I was much younger and more foolish, and my son, Ames, was just four years old, I thought it would be a capital idea to bring him along on the ride with me. Back then we didn't have the fancy equipment for hauling kids that you find now. Nowadays there are Cadillac trailers, enclosed with their own ecosystem, for the little tykes. They come equipped with the very best in sound systems and DVD players so the little urchins don't get bored. The best I could come up with was a child carrier seat strapped on the back of my bike and a plastic bag of cheerios which Ames dropped before we'd gone two miles. We set out in the morning with what equipment I could carry, but knowing that sixty miles was a long way to carry a little kid. Lots of things could go wrong.

They did.

Around midday the rain began. We had no rain gear. There was no shelter on the bike for my poor son, who happened to hate the outdoor elements with a passion. I didn't get a mile in the rain before he was in absolute hysterics. I stopped at the side of the road, rain pouring down in sheets, and huddled over him as best I could. But he was inconsolable. I wasn't too happy myself. We couldn't ride under these conditions. So I pulled off and took shelter in a nearby barn, where Ames dried off a little and warmed up. Soon he was running around in the hay, chasing wild kittens. So that was good. But the hours were passing, we weren't getting any closer to our destination, and the rain wasn't letting up. It took me another hour to beg, plead, order, bribe, and generally manhandle Ames back into that bike seat so we could get back on the road. We finished the rest of the ride not speaking, Ames in tears and me with grim determination.

When we came in sight of his mother at the campsite waiting for us, Ames burst into tears again. I got him out of the seat and he ran to her, lamenting, "I need a hug!" Ann looked at me accusingly, demanding to know what I had done to her son. Nobody seemed to care that I was wet and cold, too. And I had had to do all the work. Ames would never again get into that bike seat.

But now he rides RAGBRAI like a trooper, joining in whenever he gets a chance. Kids and family on RAGBRAI are a tradition for many. I started my two children (after that awful year in the attached seat) in a trailer I pulled behind me. Over the years I added improvements like a retractable canopy for sun and rain protection. Eventually they graduated to riding a few miles on their own little bikes, and then the whole week with me. Going up hills I'd put my hand in the small of their back and sprint. It gave us great pride to pass other cyclists struggling on the hill. My daughter, Caitlin, now a junior in college, has made a complete transition. She finally owns a good road bike—one which puts to shame all the bikes I've ever owned—and she rides strongly at a racing pace. It pains me to admit she can dust her old man now. But what a sense of reward to have produced a genetic copy of myself who enjoys cycling as much as I do. My son feels the same way, though, being out of college now, he has the working man's blues and can rarely get the week off anymore. One of life's great tragedies. We're planning a family RAGBRAI family reunion next summer. I hope it plays out.

So bad things happen out there on the road, but for all the adversity I've encountered, from hills to accidents to headwinds and heat, I keep going back. Why do you suppose that is? What is this propensity that humans have for forgetting the bad times? It's fortunate that we do, otherwise most of us would never get out of bed in the morning. What woman would ever give birth to more than one child, for example? Most women I know, at the moment of childbirth, vow they're never going through that again. But babies keep on being born. And we keep returning to RAGBRAI.

Watching RAGBRAI roll by is a dizzying treat. It's like watching a parade on fast forward. It's almost hypnotizing. A steady stream of bright colors, shapes, and sizes. Kids stand by the side of the street holding out their hands for a high-five from the riders. Others sit there with their super soakers waiting for targets to whiz by. Some cycling teams toss beads to the crowds like a Mardi Gras parade. Often when you spot road-kill on the highway—a raccoon or possum that had been struck by a car maybe the night before—these teams will have put a garland of beads around its little neck as a sign of respect. Once I arrived in an overnight town very early in the morning and decided, since I had nothing better to do, to sit on the curb with local residents and be a RAGBRAI bystander. I watched a steady stream of cyclists go by for over five hours. And then I got tired of that and went to find a piece of pie and a drink. But the riders were still coming in. It's nonstop until well after dark.

The sounds of the ride are also bizarre. Riders carry horns and whistles and duck calls and trumpets, and brazenly honk and blow and blare from the middle of the peloton (the pack of riders). Loud professional-quality sound systems roll by blaring everything from heavy metal to Sinatra. In the rare moments when the peloton is quiet, the whir of tires on the road and clicking of gears is distinctive.

Aside from the riding across idyllic Grant Wood countryside, the thing most passionately enjoyed by those who participate in RAGBRAI is the small-town hospitality and local entertainment that greets the mobs along the ride. In town squares and on flatbed trucks parked in the street and city park amphitheaters, local entertainment shows up and entertains the throngs. You'll hear everything from local high school choir members trying to sing karaoke to some of the best blues bands in the Midwest. There's hardly a better feeling in the world than sitting under a tree after a long day's workout, with a cold beer in your hand, listening to good (or even bad) music. It's finally cool and you're feeling the glow of a good day's work. Or maybe it's just the beer. Whatever, it just feels good.

Downtown in these small towns, it becomes a carnival of food booths and stands selling a wild assortment of goods and services. Of course the bike shops are out. They have their own section under tarps and tents for selling tee shirts, bike parts, cycling clothing, and doing nonstop repair. A delightful assortment of tee shirts is printed up each year, and riders vie for the right souvenir. Food stands will fill the streets around the town square. Besides the local churches selling sit-down meals of chicken or spaghetti or beef and noodles in their air-conditioned basements, you can pick up almost anything your heart desires under the canopies downtown. There are hamburgers and pork burgers, corn on the cob, giant turkey legs, funnel cakes, snow cones, corn dogs, and pizza. Most of us try to sample at least a little of everything. Local people from miles around come into town to have a little dinner, drink a little beer, and gawk at the spandex-clad strangers who have taken over their town. When I stay with local families, it's fun to wander downtown with them and see this display through their eyes.

Appetites at last satisfied, at least for a couple of hours, it's time to enjoy the fruits of your labors and find a spot to crash on the grass to listen to the night's entertainment. Towns may sport two or three venues, depending on the size of the town, with a different style of music at each. You can hear big band, country and western, blues, classic rock, and sometimes all of it at the same time if the venues are close enough together.

The day spent, it's finally time to enjoy the rejuvenation of sleep. Most of us don't last much past nine or ten o'clock. It's embarrassing to think of yourself as a party animal and then have to excuse yourself at 9:30 to go brush your teeth and hit the sack. Aging is not for the faint of heart. One of my favorite RAGBRAI tee shirts reads, "The older I get, the better I was." We're stumbling over tent stakes and ropes, trying to find our own tent. But they all look alike in the dark, and darned if I can remember where I pitched mine. There are hilarious stories, some of them true I'm sure, about people crawling into the wrong sleeping bag in the wrong tent.

Those who do stay out late tend to alienate the whole campground these days. One time my mother-in-law came along as support crew for my little group. She drove the motor home and fixed meals. One night the camp ground was so noisy with late-night revelers that even in the camper we were having trouble sleeping. The most offensive tent didn't quiet down until three in the morning, giving us just two hours of uninterrupted sleep. But my mother-in-law had the last word. As soon as we cyclists left at the crack of dawn, she took her set of pots and pans over to the revelers' tent and started banging them together with all her might. "Time to get up!!!" she hollered into the screening of the tent. Without waiting for a reply, she packed up the camper and left, feeling very satisfied with herself. I saw her in a whole new light after I heard that story.

But wait, there's an even better story. This one comes to me third hand, and the perpetrator is deceased, so I make no claims about its veracity. A retired minister from my former congregation, Porter French, once told this one to a youth group gathering where he was a chaperone. Porter was eighty years old at the time of the incident. An accomplished cyclist, Porter was camping on RAGBRAI one year when, late into the night, a young couple in a tent near his was having an—shall we say—amorous night of it. A very loud amorous night, as Porter told it. Porter, something of a character, climbed out of his sleeping bag in his underwear, marched over to the tent where the indiscrete couple was carrying on, and announced so that the whole camp ground could hear, "If you two don't quiet down in there, I'm going to climb into that sleeping bag with you!" It was quiet the rest of the night.

RAGBRAI is a community on wheels. The town of Mapleton got it right. In 1981 when RAGBRAI rolled through, someone there posted a sign saying, "Welcome to RAGBRAI, Iowa—the only city in the state that can claim as its boundaries the Missouri River on the west and the Mississippi River on the east."[5]

This rolling community comes complete with everything a small town of ten or fifteen thousand would have if it weren't snaking down the highways. There's the sanitation department, providing porta-potties and drinking water and big empty refrigerator boxes for garbage. There are nomadic restaurants that pull up stakes every day and roll along with the bikes, in addition to the local clubs and church booths that pop up on every corner. There's security. A whole crew of state patrol officers moves along with the group every day, combining forces with local law enforcement in the counties we pass through. RAGBRAI isn't an unruly group. Most of the security work has to do with traffic control. There's information, repair, hospitality, whatever a rider might need. Some of it is provided by the *Des Moines Register* RAGBRAI organization, but much of it nowadays simply appears. The growth of this annual enterprise has always taken its organizers by surprise. They no longer even attempt to control or manage it; they just try to steer it as best they can in positive ways. It's like trying to deal with a runaway snowball as it careens down a hill gathering speed and size. Even if they suddenly called a halt to the whole thing, thousands of intrepid riders would show up and attempt the ride on their own.

Donald Kaul once summarized a spiritual quality of RAGBRAI.

> There is a more positive side to the ride, there's a sense of community about it, a shared experience, which is rare in contemporary life. There is a reality to it. You're not watching other people do something. You're doing something yourself. In a society that seems to be suffocating in vicarious experience, even pain can be a virtue.[6]

People get married on RAGBRAI. To my great disappointment I've never been asked to perform one of the ceremonies, but most every year there's a well-publicized wedding ceremony in a city park, with the wedding party all clad in spandex. It sounds so romantic. People meet on the ride, they find they have much in common, they strike up a relationship, and, wham, the next thing you know they're saying "I do" in front of ten thousand sweaty revelers.

I was party to one romantic connection that culminated in a wedding, though the wedding did not take place on RAGBRAI itself. My oldest and dearest biking buddy, Craig, brought a friend with him for the ride one year. The friend happened to be a woman who liked biking as much as he did. Craig and I had started bicycling together when we were seventh-grade classmates. At first the rides were to the next little town, ten miles down the road, for picnics in the park. Then we did overnight bicycle camping tours to state parks within a sixty or seventy mile radius. Our first overnight camping trip was a seventy-mile jaunt the summer after seventh grade. Today, we can't believe our parents ever let us do it. We would never let our own kids take off on an adventure like that. But no harm came to us, so we kept riding together. Finally we pulled off a thousand mile tour around the Midwest. And then came RAGBRAI every year.

Then Craig crashed the party by bringing this woman. Joyce was her name. I couldn't believe his nerve. But she was nice and she fit in well with our little group and she could keep up, so I tolerated her. It was only fair, I reasoned. I had cut our thousand mile Midwest bike tour short that summer thirty years ago in order to spend more time with my fiancée. Maybe he was trying to get back at me after all these years. I was honored when he called up later during the year after that ride and asked me to officiate at their wedding. Romance had blossomed. Today Craig and Joyce are still together and still biking. She can come back if she wants to. I guess.

No description of RAGBRAI would be complete without mention of the Pork Chop Man. One of the shared common experiences of the ride, for everyone who has been on it since 1985, is coming up a long hill somewhere out in the middle of nowhere and hearing from off in the distance ahead the cry of the ruby faced pork chop vendor: "POOOOOOOOOOORRKKK CHHHOOOOOOOOOOOOOOPPPSS! I DON'T CARE IF YOU'RE HOT AND SWEATY! I'VE GOT YOUR PORK CHOPS READY!" Paul Bernhard is the Pork Chop Man. He drives an old pink school bus, painted to look like a pig, sets up huge fire pits fueled by cast off corn cobs by the side of the road, and then he sits there and hawks his signature item. Pork chops. That's right. For six or seven bucks you can sit in the hot sun in the gravel on the shoulder of the highway chewing on greasy, tender, inch-thick Iowa chops. And you know what's funny? They're terrific! You have never tasted anything so good. You might not think that a greasy hunk of meat would be the proper fuel for a day of cycling, but you would be surprised.

There have been problems with RAGBRAI. I paint too rosy a picture if I don't mention these. Every year there are reports of drinking getting out of hand, of sexual liberties, of topless mud slides and the like. Every once in awhile a local downtown will get trashed, with broken bottles all over the street and a few souls arrested for disorderly conduct. It has been said at various times over the years that such behavior will ruin the ride; families will no longer feel safe taking part. That would be a shame.

But I have never seen this type of incident firsthand. And I've been looking, believe me. Maybe I just go to bed too early or ride too steadily during the day to see what goes on at the end of the trail. But I guess any good thing can be spoiled when done to excess.

In thirty-four years of RAGBRAI, more than a quarter million cyclists have participated, for at least part of the week. The ride has covered sixteen thousand miles. It has swelled to twenty or twenty-five thousand cyclists on days that enter or depart from some of Iowa's larger cities. And it has crisscrossed the state of Iowa, rolling through more than 750 towns, representing 78 percent of the incorporated towns in Iowa, and passing through all of Iowa's ninety-nine counties. Participants come from every state in the union (one year no one from Rhode

Island had registered, so the organizers offered an all-expense-paid RAGBRAI experience to a representative from that state). People come from around the world to see what this great ride is all about.

More than two hundred other bicycle rides throughout the United States have been inspired by RAGBRAI. It has become a worldwide attraction, with coverage in such newspapers as the *New York Times*, the *Wall Street Journal*, the *Christian Science Monitor*, and the *Miami Herald*. It has graced the pages of *Sports Illustrated*, *TIME*, *Reader's Digest*, *National Geographic's Traveler*, *Saturday Evening Post*, and *Bicycling*. In 2005, *Sports Illustrated* named RAGBRAI one of the twenty-five Summer Essentials, things you just had to do.[7]

RAGBRAI is a rolling carnival on twenty thousand wheels. RAGBRAI is a community that stretches from one side of the state of Iowa to the other during the last full week in July every year. RAGBRAI is an accident that turned into one of the best things ever to happen to Iowa. And, for our purposes here, RAGBRAI is a rich gold mine of meaning. Daily adventures on RAGBRAI are a microcosm of larger issues that play out in life. RAGBRAI provides a nonthreatening starting point from which to launch a critical observation of life as we know it. In that regard, it's a unique lens through which to examine our curious customs and habits as a people.

Or maybe it's none of this. Maybe this book is just an excuse for me to reflect on my favorite summer pastime months before I actually get to ride it. Humor me.

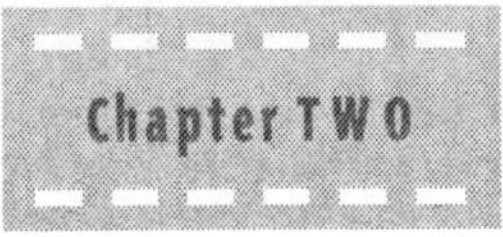

It's Not about the Destination

MANY PEOPLE today seem to think that getting somewhere in particular is the goal of life. They're impatient to arrive. They want answers and they want things settled. Open-ended journeys and questions make them uncomfortable. This type of temperament doesn't do well on RAGBRAI. I know this for a fact, because I tend toward this personality type. On the Myers-Briggs Type Indicator, I'm off the scale toward the "judgment" side on the "judging-perceiving" continuum, which means that ambiguity makes me crazy. I "choose closure over open options." I "have a sense of ease and satisfaction" upon making a decision. I "report a sense of urgency until I have made a pending decision."[8] I need things nailed down.

Part of the reason I always tend to ride so hard is so that I can get into town early, gauge the lay of the land, study town maps, set up my tent or meet my host family or check into my hotel, find where I'm going to eat, take my shower, lay out my bed, and get any other logistical uncertainties out of the way before it gets late. One night after I was all settled in and had gone downtown to scope out the local entertainment, I came across one of my friends just riding into town, all his gear on his bike, at 10 p.m. I asked him where he was going to sleep. Where was he going to find a bathroom for the night? Where was he going to brush his teeth? He said he didn't know. But neither was he worried. He'd find some place. He always did. The thought of doing a week of RAGBRAI like that horrified me.

But RAGBRAI teaches that life is not a destination but a journey. I may be off the "judging" scale in terms of personality temperament, but I can recognize the value in being open. There may be more value in living with the ambiguity of open questions than there is in rushing to answers. I'm still trying to learn that lesson. I miss a lot on RAGBRAI by always being prepared. My laid-back friend is open to whatever comes along. The destination doesn't really concern him.

On RAGBRAI, no one in his or her right mind would pour out the energy and face the sacrifices of biking four hundred or five hundred miles in the dead of summer in Iowa just to get from, say, Sergeant Bluff to Muscatine. Take the bus, for heaven's sake. Or better yet, stay home and watch the coverage on TV. There's just no intrinsic reason to go to Muscatine or Sabula or Bellevue or Fort Madison or Dubuque. Arriving at the Mississippi River on Saturday after cycling for seven days is probably the biggest letdown of the week. The boat ramps are always hot and crowded and you're tired and cranky, and have you ever actually seen the Mississippi? It's muddy and it stinks and it's full of unidentifiable brown things roiling around in it. We rode all this way just for this?! Once I thought it would be a real kick to just ride my bike right on into the river as a fitting end to the week. Bad idea. I was cleaning goo out of my bicycle gears for a month, and I had to burn my clothes. Then I got this funny rash. In short, the river itself is no destination. The fun was all in the getting there. Not the arrival.

Arriving at the end of the ride is not just anticlimactic. It's depressing. Arriving signals the end of this glorious week. It leaves riders with an empty feeling. We've been pouring our energy into riding and eating and camaraderie, and now it's over. The community that had been assembled over the course of the week begins to dissolve. Maybe you'll see a few carloads of RAGBRAI riders at the truck stop on the interstate on the way home. You'll exchange greetings and wish one another well until next year, and then they're gone and you have nothing to do but return to your life. One year at the end of the ride, organizer John Karras relates that he fell into a dangerous and surprising clinical depression. "I found myself staring over a precipice into the black hole of depression. The emotional buildup had been incredible. Then it was over. Done. Talking about it with me years later, Kaul said, 'It was tough going back to being just a communist,' to which I replied, 'It was even tougher going back to the night copydesk.'"[9] His feelings, though extreme, are understandable. We have all shared them, to one degree or another.

RAGBRAI is about riding, not getting there. My older brother, who has joined us on RAGBRAI just twice in all these years, got it right, though it pains me to have to admit it. I still like to get on my bike and ride. I tend to put my head down and crank hard and steady to see how fast I can cover the miles. He likes to stop and play. Once when he was with me we stopped at a farmstead for homemade root beer floats. They were wonderfully refreshing as we dawdled under the shade of a tree in the front yard of this farm house. "Yes, Bill," I grudgingly had to admit, "it was a good idea to stop." Now I was set for another twenty or thirty miles of riding. But then, as we mounted our bikes and rolled back onto the highway, we hadn't gone thirty yards before he spied a small sign advertising free beer on the other side of the road. So he pulled in there, too. Turned out there was not only free beer, but a mud slide and a wet tee shirt competition (Bill won), and it was the highlight of the day.

I recall one day back in the mid-1990s when I was riding out of my type-A personality. Back then I still considered myself a gonzo rider. My workout and racing friend, Austin, and I started the day's ride hammering for speed and endurance. We kept encountering pace lines and jumping in. A pace line is a group of riders traveling in close configuration, like the Blue Angels in formation, each one drafting off the one ahead and thereby saving up to 30 percent of their energy output. The lead rider will take a turn at the front, in effect pulling the whole group along, and then he or she will drift off the lead toward the back to save energy until it's his or her turn to lead again. A group of tightly organized cyclists can ride considerably faster than any of them could alone. Drafting is a key piece of strategy in any bike race. So Austin and I were chasing down draft lines and occasionally even smashing them by setting too fast a pace for the other riders. It was great, a display of manly testosterone without anyone having to die.

But I got really tired of this after a while. After a pull at the front, I simply drifted off the back and coasted awhile, letting the group disappear over a hill. I lifted my head up and looked around. There were trees, crops, hills and valleys, farmsteads, and other cyclists I hadn't even noticed before. It was quite a change of perspective. Soon the road came to a lake, following the shore for a mile or two. There was a dock off the side of the road, and several cyclists had stopped there to jump in and cool off. I didn't have anything better to do at the moment, so I joined them. You can't imagine how refreshing it is to slide under the surface of the cool water, even in a muddy Iowa pond, on a hot day when you've been racing all day. The tension in your body melts. After I got out of the lake and had drip dried a bit on the dock in the sun, I got back on my bike and slowly wheeled into our day's destination.

I found Austin. He was pumped up with stories about hanging with pace lines and destroying weaker riders. I said, "Austin, I had a great day. That lake was just perfect. I got off and went for a swim."

He said, "What lake?"

Life is in the distractions. God created us to enjoy the beauty of this world, not to simply put up with it until we are taken to a "better place." I say, don't let this place we're at now get away. God made it and, at the end of the day, God pronounced it "good." If it's good enough for God, it's good enough for us. If we don't enjoy this world, we're not going to enjoy the one to come. We're not called to wait for the "end time" in order to be raptured. We're called to engage as fully as possible in the present and infuse it with all the passion we can. No one, at the end of his or her life, ever wishes he or she had made more money, or accomplished more, or climbed higher on the corporate ladder. Or ridden their bike faster. At least, no one that I've ever sat with during their dying moments. They don't lie there wishing they'd "arrived." No, if they lament anything, it's that they hadn't spent more time with their kids, or taken more adventures, or said "I love you" more often to their spouse, or played more. People at the end of their lives consistently wish they had enjoyed the journey more. They think of the swimming holes they missed along the way.

When I take church youth groups across the country on mission trips, I generally follow interstates in order to get to my day's destination as fast as possible. But on my last trip, to North Carolina, we had in tow my farmer friend, Barney, driving his big white pickup truck in our caravan of five vehicles. Barney can't stand interstates. After two days of driving at the end of our line on four-lane divided highways, Barney suddenly decided he'd had enough. He snatched the lead and took off overland, daring the rest of us to follow. It wasn't even a "blue highway" he'd taken us down. It was a country lane that didn't even appear on my map. But on his little excursion we discovered a picturesque covered bridge and found a local restaurant where some of our group ate grits for the first time in their lives. Barney has a back-roads cross-country tour lined up for me if I can ever find the time to go with him. He's convinced it will do me good. I'm going to get a GPS tracking device before I go.

Not everyone is comfortable with the ambiguity and uncertainty that journeys entail. I think there are two kinds of people in the world: destination thinkers and journey thinkers. This distinction could go a long way toward accounting for the great cultural divide our country seems to be experiencing today. Some people seem driven toward certainty. They don't want to set out on a journey of unpredictability. Journeys are risky so they want to stay "home." Destination thinkers want things nailed down, clear, concrete. They want rules on how to behave. They think there's already too much in flux; they prefer a condition they consider as safe. They're into defining things and setting boundaries. Like who is in and who is out, what is right and what is wrong. Then they want to legislate these certainties so that people who are different are either coerced into conformity or made to desist—or, better yet, simply disappear.

The ecumenical movement among Christians was a powerful force in the middle of the last century. It brought many denominations together to work on common issues. The National Council of Churches and the World Council of Churches are both expressions of the ecumenical movement. But ecumenism is a bad word for fundamentalist Christians. Ecumenism entails sitting across the table from people you may not agree with. Fundamentalists, who by definition tend to believe that they are in the right and therefore everyone else is wrong, don't feel the need to consort with those who disagree with them. The ecumenical movement is in decline today as more and more people gravitate toward the extremes of certainty.

Those who focus on the destination build defensible perimeters with which they can keep out those who have alternative answers or lifestyles or religions.

Those who focus on the journey wander around and explore. It is rightly said, "Not all who wander are lost." Barney may have been off the map, but he is never lost.

Those who focus on the destination circle the wagons. They build fortresses and walls and moats. These are the people who are busy erecting a fence at the Mexican border (using billions of taxpayer dollars that might otherwise have gone into employment or equal access to healthcare or education or ongoing Hurricane Katrina relief—the kinds of things Jesus talked about) to keep out foreigners. "Illegals," they call them (as opposed to "human beings desperate for a better life"). They feel the need to "defend our way of life" from encroachment from the South. They want to protect, at all cost, their "Truth" from all who are different, and therefore threatening.

Those who focus on the journey don't make fences, they make discoveries. They pick up useful trinkets along the way. They might be transformed by what they encounter. They look forward to the possibility of transformation. Transformation isn't exactly a desirable outcome for destination thinkers. Change is a bad word for those who focus on destinations. Change implies a watering down of their Truth. Reality is black and white for those focused on destinations. Out on the journey, it's all gray.

There are destination-thinkers scattered all through the Bible. There were many Hebrews who actively complained to Moses all the way across the desert, like demanding, self-centered children, "Are we there yet? Are we there yet? Are we there yet?" They complained that they were hungry and thirsty. Even when God provided manna, they said they missed meat. Never mind that they were fleeing oppression and starvation. Never mind that they were slowly making their way toward a promised land flowing with milk and honey. They got scared and wanted to go back to the "good old days" of slavery. It's not commonly known because few people read the original Hebrew anymore, but it is recorded in the most ancient of manuscripts that God scolded them, saying, "If I have to stop this Exodus and come back there, you kids are going to be in big trouble!"

Much later, the disciples of Jesus got trapped in the same thinking. Peter, John, and James went up with Jesus to a mountain, where he was "transfigured." Moses and Elijah appeared with him. What did the disciples want to do? Build a worship site. Construct a monument. Stay put. But what did Jesus demand of them? Return to the valley and get back to the work of mission: healing the sick, teaching seekers, feeding the hungry.

Pharaoh was one of those destination people. He demanded rigid conformity and was threatened by diversity. His kind always keeps order through power and intimidation. Caesar was a destination kind of guy. Everything had to be done his way. When Jesus came along proposing an alternative to the Roman system of domination, that Roman system had no choice but to eliminate him.

Fear may be a strong influence behind the quest for certainty and stability that drives many people today. We fear we are in a world gone crazy, with too few standards and no agreed-upon rules. The world used to be predictable, they lament. (Is that so?, I wonder.) We were all on the same page. (Were we? And if so, what was that page?) We knew the role of women, people of color, gays and lesbians, foreigners. Wars were fought face to face. There were standards of behavior. But have you seen the nightly news lately? It's full of murders and rapes, suicide bombings and school hostage situations. Social roles that used to be predictable are all in flux. Conservative voters long for the imagined good old days when values weren't so relative. They're trying to protect an ordered society from what must seem like barbaric hordes encamped outside the gates. Fundamentalism, as we experience it today, is a reaction against what is perceived as widespread secular humanism rising out of the post-enlightenment western scientific mindset. It's an almost anti-intellectual attempt to return to a more ordered world of predictable Newtonian physics. Never mind the weight of evidence for the scientific theory of evolution. Evolution seems to conflict with a literal reading of the creation accounts in Genesis. So it must be wrong. But can you ever really go back to *not knowing* what we now know about the world?

I can empathize with this concern. It's intimidating to think that your cherished values have been abandoned by modern society. Who's in charge? Whatever happened to objective truth?

But this fear, which is a natural human response to change and uncertainty, is often manipulated by those who seek power. President George W. Bush got a blank check from Congress and the American people to declare a preemptive war on a country that had absolutely nothing to with the 9/11 terrorist attacks because we were, as a nation, uniquely unified by fear in those early days after the attacks. Fearful voters can be rallied to the polls by appealing to the threat to their "way of life" allegedly posed by the prospect of same-sex marriage. Political strategists from both major political parties are well aware of the power of fear. It's hard to imagine a stronger motivating force.

Just as setting out on RAGBRAI is no fun if you're fearful about what the day might bring, so no one can set out on a journey of discovery, risking growth and transformation, when bedeviled by fear such as this. Fear motivates one to retreat and react. We're pushed, so we push back. But a clenched fist can never open to receive new gifts. It can never release gifts to others. How can we overcome fear in order to journey into a promised future of hope and joy? Will more regulations help? If we can fortify ourselves more effectively will it be safe to venture out? If we can blast our enemies from our path will it be safe to step out? Of course not. What's called for is a change in paradigms. The Bible calls it conversion, a change of heart.

John says that perfect love casts out all fear. Jesus reduces Hebrew legalism down to two principles: love of God and love for others. All the rest is trivial detail. Love sets a higher standard than law. It's not that we're moving into a region of lawlessness; we're moving into a hospitable land of compassion. "I do not come to abolish the law, but to fulfill it," says Jesus. And the Bible assures us that we don't travel alone. God is a constant companion on our journey. The late William Sloane Coffin, a Yale University chaplain and outspoken advocate for justice issues, wrote:

> Rules at best are signposts, never hitching posts. Personally I doubt whether there is such a thing as a Christian rule. There are probably only acts that are more or less Christian depending on the motives prompting them. . . .
>
> In short, we have come up with love as an answer to legalism on the one hand and lawlessness on the other. Love hallows individuality. Love consecrates and never desecrates personality. Love demands that all our actions reflect a movement toward and not away from nor against each other. And love insists that all people assume their responsibility for all their relations.[10]

Back in one community where I was a pastor, the son of one of my parishioners was dating the daughter of a conservative pastor in town. Now, we were on good terms, this pastor and I.

We met regularly through the local ministerial association and collaborated on common mission projects like the local Crop Walk and Habitat for Humanity. So I was surprised to learn that, although it was perfectly acceptable for the young man from my church to attend this other pastor's church with his daughter, his daughter was expressly forbidden to visit my church. Apparently we weren't Christian enough, or we weren't the right kind of Christians, or our message was tainted somehow. We did preach a radical message of inclusion at my church. We openly announced that all were welcome. During my tenure we voted to become "open and affirming," spelling out that all marginalized persons—including gays and lesbians—were welcome into the full life and ministry of the church. I guess if a message of radical hospitality got Jesus killed, it could still be threatening today to people who make judgments and draw boundaries.

One crucial aspect of Jesus' itinerant ministry was his deliberate and intimate attention to people regarded by his society as marginal. He openly spoke with women, including those of questionable morals, which was against the rules of the day, and he allowed children into his teachings. He touched the sick, the dead, and the dying, which would have rendered him ritualistically impure by Jewish standards of the day. He consorted with sinners rather than confining himself to the holy. He even tended to Romans. He picked grain on the Sabbath day of rest when his disciples were hungry, and healed sick people on holy days when the keepers of the law forbade it. The central identifying feature of the ministry of Jesus was breaking down social, ecclesiastical, and political barriers in order to establish relationships of compassion. He wasn't into defending righteousness, he was into relationships. How do we imagine that reconstructing those old barriers of doctrine and dogma could ever be a faithful response to the way of Jesus?

Coffin spoke clearly about the danger of doctrines:

> It is bad religion to deify doctrines and creeds. . . . Doctrines, let's not forget, supported slavery and apartheid; some still support keeping women in their places and gays

> and lesbians in limbo. Moreover, doctrines can divide while compassion can only unite. In other words, religious folk, all our lives, have both to recover tradition and to recover from it.[11]

Destination thinkers can be dangerous people. If they are self-righteous and arrogant they have a tendency to define themselves as right and everyone else as wrong. Coffin, again, writes, "With spiritual arrogance goes the itch to destroy. History warns that the best is always a hair's breadth from the worst, and that heartless moralists in the corridors of power are those who start inquisitions."[12]

People who were certain about their own faith and salvation crashed airliners into the World Trade Center towers and the Pentagon on 9/11. Since they "knew" they were going to heaven, they were confident their "enemies" were going to hell. People who were certain about the superiority of their race and culture exterminated six million Jews during the 1940s in Germany. They defined Judaism as a virus and then they set about to "cure" the body. People who were certain about their views of God led the Crusades and the Inquisition. Contemporary biblical scholar and popular lecturer Marcus J. Borg claims "theology has always been bedeviled by the quest for excessive certitude."[13]

Certainty, played out in fundamentalism, is the greatest threat facing the world today. Many of us are rightly concerned about terrorism or weapons of mass destruction or the imperialistic aims of powerful countries. But these issues, important as they are in understanding global instability, are not at the heart of the matter. It's what lies behind those issues. The greatest threat to world security and God's vision of the peaceable kingdom are fundamentalists—Christian, Muslim, Jewish, economic, political, nationalistic, or any other form—who are so certain of their own rightness that they see everyone else as wrong and therefore expendable. We have a global conflict brewing today between fundamentalists of different faiths. Those who are convinced that they have sole access to the

Truth put the rest of the world at risk when they attempt to enforce their dogmatism.

Former president Jimmy Carter warns:

> There is a remarkable trend toward fundamentalism in all religions—including the different denominations of Christianity as well as Hinduism, Judaism and Islam.
>
> Increasingly, true believers are inclined to begin a process of deciding: "Since I am aligned with God, I am superior and my beliefs should prevail, and anyone who disagrees with me is inherently wrong," and the next step is "inherently inferior." The ultimate step is "subhuman," and then their lives are not significant.
>
> That tendency has created, throughout the world, intense religious conflicts. Those Christians who resist the inclination toward fundamentalism and who truly follow the nature, actions, and words of Jesus Christ should encompass people who are different from us with our care, generosity, forgiveness, compassion, and unselfish love.
>
> It is not easy to do this. It is a natural human inclination to encapsulate ourselves in a superior fashion with people who are just like us—and to assume that we are fulfilling the mandate of our lives if we just confine our love to our own family or to people who are similar and compatible. Breaking through this barrier and reaching out to others is what personifies a Christian and what emulates the perfect example that Christ set for us.[14]

Fundamentalism arises when we miss the point of our faith. Religion is supposed to be a way of life that unites, not a set of principles that divides. Marcus J. Borg writes:

> Christianity is about a way of life, a path, and it has been from its very beginning. At the center of Jesus' own teaching is the notion of a "way" or a "path," and the first name of the early Christian movement was "the Way."[15]

There's plenty of biblical evidence for this view. God's people are always being called away from home and family and the familiar to follow God into unknown adventures. Abraham and Sarah had to pick up their tent stakes and move their extended family from Iraq to Palestine. We think covering seventy or eighty miles a day by bicycle is challenging. They were moving an entire tribe, along with flocks and herds. A couple of miles a day was probably all they could manage. And there weren't any lemonade stands or pork burgers for sale along the route. At the end of it all their faithfulness was "reckoned to them as righteousness." It wasn't about believing, it was about following. The Hebrews enslaved in Egypt were liberated by Moses and then spent the next forty years wandering around in the desert wondering where they were going and who was in charge. Moses would have appreciated another of my favorite RAGBRAI tee shirts, which reads, "Which way did they go? How many of them were there? How fast were they going? I must find them. I am their leader." The wandering, following, trusting theme occurs over and over again in the Bible.

The life of Jesus provides another example. Jesus did not stake a claim to a piece of territory or dogma or moral principle and just sit there defending it. Jesus was constantly on the move. He roamed around the countryside with his disciples, speaking to people, entering homes, taking boat trips, going fishing. "As they were going along the road, someone said to him, 'I will follow you wherever you go.' And Jesus said to him, 'Foxes have holes and birds of the air have nests, but the Son of Man has nowhere to lay his head'" (Luke 9:57-58). He was an itinerant preacher. Those who were converted to his cause didn't just go to church, they left their families and their fishing nets to follow him all over the countryside. Jesus and his crew traveled from town to town teaching, healing, casting out demons, feeding the hungry, and bringing the dead back to life, until the road ended on a cross in Jerusalem. And even then, after Jesus' death, the disciples were flung out into the world and through history, always on the move, always following this open-ended pilgrimage of faith. Jesus' entire ministry was a movement through the world closing in on the mystery of full communion with God.

Bishop John Shelby Spong calls Christians to be less concerned about the right answers than about finding the right path to pursue. In a video series for Christian seekers called *Living the Questions*, Spong says that the Christian life is a journey into the mystery of God. We never arrive, but are constantly pushing against boundaries. Those who believe they have arrived are not, in their certainty, better Christians than those of us who still raise questions about faith. In fact, he says the certain ones are idolaters. They have stopped worshiping the mystery of God and have focused instead on their own version of God's truth.[16] They have created a golden calf out of their personal perspective; they bow down and worship this thing of their own creation rather than the holy mystery of God. Faith takes a little humility. We might just be wrong about things. We might not have all the answers. We might not have the final version of truth. In a postmodern world, we must acknowledge that there may be no such thing as a final version of truth.

The United Church of Christ has recently launched a new identity campaign, central to which is the claim that "God is still speaking." We quote Gracie Allen, the wife of George Burns, who left a message for her husband saying, "Never put a period where God has placed a comma." Lest you think my church listens only to entertainers, one of our forebears in the faith, Pastor John Robinson, sent his Pilgrim flock on their way to the New World with the words, "There is yet more light and truth to break forth from God's holy word." Gracie Allen just came up with her own way of expressing that truth. If it is true that God is still speaking, then any claim to possess the truth, the whole truth, and nothing but the truth, so help me God, is false. We have yet more to learn from experience in the world and our encounter with the Divine. The "Still Speaking" campaign may be unique to the UCC, but the message is one that will be recognized and resonate within progressive elements in all the major historic denominations. There is a sense among many faithful disciples and scholars that our versions of the truth must always be tentative and conditional.

I don't think God expects rigid conformity from us. God welcomes people from varieties of paths, points of view, and perspectives. All humans are created in the image of God, the creation narrative claims, not just those who agree on certain fine points of dogma. When Jesus said, "I am the way," he wasn't denying the legitimacy of other spiritual journeys. If God were in charge of RAGBRAI it would be absolute chaos—I mean even more chaotic than it is today—because cyclists would be approaching the Mississippi River from every which way. Some of them might end up in an entirely different place—they might find themselves in Minnesota or Missouri.

Actually, my friend Rich already rides RAGBRAI that way (although I can't say with absolute certainty that he has ever ended up in Minnesota or Missouri—not that he would be opposed to such a thing). While most of us throw our luggage on the trucks and meet up with our group every night, Rich rides with full camping gear on his bike so he can pitch his tent anywhere that tickles his fancy. One year he rode with a giant bongo drum strapped on top of his gear so he could play it at night. His flowing curly hair billows out from under his helmet—when he can be bothered to wear a helmet. Rich never rides the official RAGBRAI route, either. He likes to take side roads to see where they lead. Sometimes you'll see him backtracking along the route to go see something he missed. Sometimes you won't see Rich all week, until we all meet up at the charter bus. And sometimes, not even then. Rich finds his own way. Nobody understands Rich, and that's just the way he seems to like it. He's the epitome of RAGBRAI.

Another classic RAGBRAI tee shirt reads, "Where are we going? And what's with this hand basket?"

Tex Sample, popular commentator on the faith scene in contemporary American life, tells a story about the Santa Fe Trail that illustrates this point. At one point in his life he moved to Kansas City. Being something of a history buff, he was interested in seeing the Santa Fe Trail, which passes through there.

He had always imagined it to be a couple of deeply worn wagon wheel ruts carved into the prairie soil as countless families pressed west. He was surprised to find there were places in the broad valleys of Kansas where the trail was six miles wide. People weren't always following the same sets of tracks. They were finding their own way west. Sample takes this as a metaphor for the Christian tradition. There is no single Christian tradition. There are tremendous varieties in faith expression and interpretation throughout the centuries. There are multiple paths—legitimate paths, each of them—to follow Christ and seek God. To define one as the correct path would be a perversion of faith.[17]

I happen to think that there's room for disagreement on almost any issue, even about strongly held faith-based affirmations. Life is less about agreeing on universally accepted conclusions or behaving according to narrowly prescribed moral principles, than it is about journeying on an open-ended path into a brighter future. And who knows where that path will lead? Knowing the answers is less important than finding a meaningful path on which to travel. Behaving in accordance to a strict code of ethics is less important than the relationships we form along the road. Nothing trumps love. I believe that God invites us on this journey and beckons to us from the future. God expects us to find our own way and to enjoy the trip in company with others.

Certainty is not a virtue of the church but a vice. Spong argues that on our journey we have to abandon every dogmatic literalization along the way—literalization of scripture and doctrine and dogma and creed. He says it is the role of pastors not to supply answers, but to shepherd the people along the way of questions. That's why his educational video series is called "Living the Questions" rather than "Giving the Answers." Travel light, Spong advises. Just take a little water along for baptisms and a little bread and wine for nourishment along the road.[18] We'll find whatever else we need out there.

Journeys are inherently risky. RAGBRAI cyclists know this. All one can know about the journey with certainty is that it will certainly get hot, though it might also get frigid. It will be hilly, you may get lost, and headwinds and rain may batter you. Tires will go flat. But never fear. There's a whole community rolling right along with you. There may not be a pillar of fire by night and a pillar of cloud by day, but there will be cold watermelon in the shade at the next city park, there will be good Samaritans to patch our bike tires, and farmers will come along to haul our bikes into town if we need a lift. They won't run out of beer, no matter how much the ones who get into town first may drink. And if they do run out, Jesus, our constant companion, will just make more. If he could turn water into wine for a wedding feast, surely he'd oblige some parched cyclists. The unknown road ahead is not scary. It's just different from the place we are now. Keep your eyes—and heart—open for what lessons God may be preparing for you. We haven't heard the last word yet.

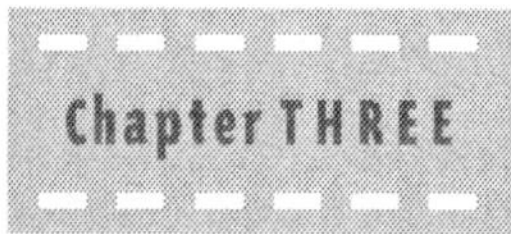

Chapter THREE

Any Way You Can with Whatever You've Got

YOU CAN see every manner of bicycle and rider on RAGBRAI. There are riders wearing loon decoys or corn cobs or antlers or toilet paper rolls attached to their helmets. There are teams wearing tutus, kilts, housedresses, and lab coats. Once I was passed by a naked guy. There are rumors to the effect that I was once or twice seen riding in a ladies' dress. But I'll deny them if confronted. And photos won't hold up in court. Photos can always be retouched. It wasn't me. That's my story, and I'm sticking to it.

You'll find cyclists on RAGBRAI riding every manner of machine, too, from slick $5,000 racing machines to $39 Huffys. There are low-slung recumbents as comfortable as lazy-boys on wheels. Some riders pull trailers with giant sound systems behind them. One guy used to pull a canoe with his camping gear in it. There are tandems, tri's, and a couple of quad bicycles with four riders mounted on top. There's always at least one gallant fellow riding an "ordinary," one of those antique bikes with the giant wheel in front and the tiny back wheel. And a few crazies do the week on unicycles or inline skates. Some people with physical disabilities ride hand-crank cycles.

I used to ride RAGBRAI way off the front of the pack, ahead of almost every other cyclist. It was a great source of pride. I was a strong recreational cyclist, dabbling in racing, and I used RAGBRAI as a training event and a chance to test my strength. I could leave town at the crack of dawn, crank hard and steady for several hours with no break at all, and pull into the next overnight town before 10 a.m., having been passed by no one. Now that I've experienced RAGBRAI at a more pedestrian pace, I can see the folly of my early standards (I missed a lot of free beer and swimming holes along the way), but I gloried in my strength and self-control.

This is a good place for me to explain the change that occurred in my life several years back. As I said, I used to be a competitive cyclist. I'm still competitive, but now I compete from the seat of a three-wheeled handcyle, powered by my arm muscles rather than legs. I have one of those handicap parking placards hanging from the rear view mirror of my car. Due to a spinal cord injury incurred a few years back, these days I use a wheelchair for daily mobility. You might be wondering why I waited until this point in the book to mention such a seemingly significant fact. My answer would be that, well, it just hasn't come up yet. That reflects my understanding of disability. It's not an issue unless it's an issue. I do many things that aren't affected in the least by my disability. The whole point of this chapter is that RAGBRAI is RAGBRAI no matter how you ride it. So participating in the ride with a disability, using adaptive technology, is no big deal. It's simply part of the wildly diverse scene out there on the road. By extension, of course, my conclusion will be that life is life no matter how you approach it. Diversity is to be accepted and honored.

Here's what happened. In May of 1997, while I was out for an early summer training ride, I was struck from behind by a truck, thrown 113 feet from my bike into the ditch by the side of the road, and left for dead by a hit-and-run driver. We can get into issues of unresolved anger and forgiveness some other time.

Fortunately there were several witnesses who rushed to my aid. No one got a license number off the truck, but they took care of me as best they could, and they got an ambulance there quickly. I was taken to the local hospital, where the doctors took one look at me and called for a helicopter to fly me to the trauma center in Des Moines. I was in surgery all that night, and infused with 56 units of blood during the operations. The surgeon later told me that he had never seen anyone so badly injured recover, but he wasn't about to give up yet. Thank God for his tenacity! It was six weeks before I woke up, and I have no recall of the accident or the ensuing weeks.

I woke up in a daze sometime around the middle of July, which was a good thing because my stupor kept me from panic when I learned the extent of my injuries. I had a tracheotomy—a breathing tube in my throat—which kept me from speaking. My kidneys had shut down, so I was wheeled down to dialysis treatments several times a week. My lower back, pelvis, and hips had been pulverized and they healed crooked. But the most serious injury was to my spinal cord. I'm paraplegic now, which means I have only limited use of my legs, and I will be in a wheelchair the rest of my life.

A new life gradually unfolded before me as I reluctantly closed the door on my old life. Learning the ropes has been the greatest challenge I've ever had to face. I was in the hospital another three months for physical therapy, gaining strength and learning the tricks of the trade necessary to roll through the world in a wheelchair. I learned to hop curbs and use escalators, although under tightened airport security since 9/11 I sometimes get yanked from airport escalators by overzealous security guards. Middle-aged balding men in wheelchairs charging up escalators apparently fit the terrorist profile somehow.

Gradually I returned to an approximation of my former life. My wife, Ann, kept urging me to consider all the options; I didn't have to go back to being a parish pastor if I didn't want to. But I could see no other life, so I clawed my way back. My generous, supportive, visionary congregation handled all the logistics. They kept me on salary as I struggled back to work. It was a year before I could maintain a full-time schedule. They also contracted with another pastor who could fill in for me during that year. It was a stressful time for them and for me, but we weathered it together.

Getting back into sports was going to be an important step. The physical therapy department in the hospital had an old upright handcycle for their patients to try out. It looked like a wheelchair on three wheels with an ice cream churn crank in front. One day as I advanced in my treatment they decided to put me on the cycle and see how I liked it. I cranked it out of the room into the hallway. That was pretty cool. Now I had a long straight stretch to gain momentum. I cranked as hard as I could while the staff ran along behind shouting warnings. I swung around a corner on two wheels and picked up speed. The wind was in my face and it felt like old times out on the roads. I had to get me one of these!

So the first thing I did the following spring was buy a handcycle. The one I ended up with was set up for racing. It has twenty-seven speeds, cantilevered back wheels for stability in cornering, and it's low to the ground for less wind resistance. The strongest riders can crank out a twenty-mile-an-hour average speed. I can do seventeen or eighteen now. But back then it was a chore just to get it moving. My first ride was a half mile out and back and I was exhausted at the end of it. But regular training has increased my strength a little every year so that I can roll with strong able-bodied recreational riders now. I like to think that I do all this training in order to make my daily life easier—I'm constantly transferring in and out of my wheelchair, which is all about upper body strength—but I've gone way beyond what you'd need to do to maintain daily fitness. I'll admit it, I'm obsessive about the exercise.

Life in a wheelchair is an adventure—not unlike RAGBRAI. I wrote a book in 2004, *Blindsided by Grace: Entering the World of Disability*,[19] about adjusting to the fact of disability. In the book I compare incurring a disability to a cross-cultural adventure in another country. Living with a disability, like living in another culture, isn't necessarily tragic or pitiful. It's just different. It may take some getting used to, but it can be managed.

What I know about cross-cultural adjustment has served me well in adapting to the culture of disability. My wife and I served in the Peace Corps in Guatemala right out of college in the late 1970s. In the early 1990s we went back to Central America, this time to Nicaragua with the Mennonite Central Committee. We had two children in tow for this latest extended excursion. Our son, Ames, was nine and our daughter, Caitlin, five.

Caitlin was not a child who relished change. We told her that three years in Nicaragua would be fun. She'd even learn Spanish. But she wasn't buying it. On our actual trip, we stopped first in Guatemala, where we would be getting a Spanish refresher course. It was a long and harrowing day of flying, what with two kids and luggage for three years. We were lugging eight checked pieces and six or eight carry-ons, including one medium-sized suitcase full of Lego blocks. We sternly warned our kids to behave when we hit the customs area of the airport. Ann and I knew how the customs officials could make life a living hell for tourists who got out of line. We could be unpacking and repacking duffel bags until midnight.

As we approached the customs line, the tension became too much for Caitlin. She burst into a full-blown tantrum. She was screaming at the top of her lungs, "I don't wanna speak Spanish!" All our hopes of evading the attention of the officials were dashed. This dysfunctional Gringo family became, in effect, the only show in town. Fortunately, the customs guys just smiled and waved us through. They knew no self-respecting terrorist would travel with a five-year-old.

When I woke up from my coma and came to realize that my legs were paralyzed, I was in the same state that my daughter was on entering Guatemala. If I could have spoken, I would have been screaming, "I don't wanna be crippled!" It was, to put it mildly, a shock.

But Caitlin, bless her heart, settled down. She made local friends in our neighborhood and at school and got her needs met. Yes, she did learn Spanish. By the time we were through with our assignment, she spoke it like a native. In fact, she's now majoring in Spanish in college and plans to spend spring semester in our old stomping grounds in Central America, studying sustainable development. She became so comfortable in that setting that she cried and carried on when it was time to leave Central America and return to Iowa.

After the initial shock, I settled down, too, and realized I would just have to learn to get around in this new culture of disability. It turned out to be not the tragedy that we all might imagine. We're always too quick to judge. How many times do we think to ourselves—if not say out loud—"Boy, if I had to be in a wheelchair I'd just kill myself"? In fact, many people with disabilities get asked that very question. Have you considered suicide? As though that were a solution to disability. We can't imagine ourselves in that situation, so we make snap judgments about how horrible it must be. We do the same thing regarding people living under difficult circumstances in foreign cultures. We jump to feelings of pity or an urge to rescue without even considering the possibility of joy being present in the situation. Adjusting to living with a disability is just different, and it takes some getting used to.

Everything changes when you start out in a wheelchair. Stairs and narrow doorways become the enemy. In fact, you'll find obstacles in places you never would have imagined. Simply opening a stubborn door takes skill, tenacity, and often luck. But the wheels make rolling through a mall on a shopping excursion with your wife or daughter a breeze. They're always looking for a place to sit down and rest. I, on the other hand, never have to stand up. People with disabilities often have to invent new ways to take care of normal bathroom routines. What we thought we had learned about pooping and peeing when we were two now has to be relearned and reinvented. I won't go into the details. I dress by flopping around in bed like a freshly caught catfish. Drives my wife crazy. You know the saying, "Well, we all put our pants on one leg at a time." I don't.

I use hand controls in my car to drive. To get into the car, I transfer into the driver's seat and then lean over and start dismantling my wheelchair. I toss the cushion into the back seat.

The wheels pop off and I place them in the passenger's side foot area. Then I heft the rigid frame over my lap between my chest and the steering wheel, and place it on the passenger's seat. I bought the car I now use for how it accommodated the chair, and for safety and reliability on the road—I can't just get out and walk to a service station if it breaks down or gets stuck in a snow drift. We bought the house we're living in now for how well it accommodated a wheelchair. Not for the ambience of the neighborhood, not for the location, but for wheelchair efficiency. Everything revolves around me being able to function. I often say that when I get out of my accessible environment, I become situationally handicapped. Motel rooms or homes or buildings or urban environments that don't accommodate my chair handicap me in ways that my normal environment doesn't. Generally speaking, I can still do most of what I did before. I just have to find different ways to get it done. Sometimes that takes massive amounts of ingenuity, perseverance, and patience. But, if it's worth the effort, I'll get it done.

RAGBRAI was worth the effort. I trained up to the distance and now crank the whole thing by hand. Hills and headwinds are always a challenge. It doesn't matter how strong I get, my arms will never be as strong as my legs were. It's frustrating to me that people who are obviously less well-trained than I am can breeze past me up the hills. Another challenge associated with handcycling is that I'm trapped on the cycle all day until I arrive at where my wheelchair has been delivered. I can't lay it down and walk around. There are no bathrooms designed to accommodate a handcycle. I can't access any toilet. I can't roll through a crowd to line up for food. I have to ask for help. I have no choice.

One rider who impressed me very much in the early years was Jon Riggs, who rode on a bike with just one pedal. He only needed one pedal because he had only one leg. He had lost his right leg to bone cancer when he was a child. Now he cycled with just a left pedal. He would hop on his bike, quickly strap his foot into the pedal, and pull away. He pedaled in a circular motion with his good leg, both pushing down and pulling up, and he rode more strongly than most able-bodied riders, even uphill. I passed him on a hill one time as he was hopping out of the ditch. It seems he had been hammering so hard on the pedal that his crank had snapped off. As you might imagine, he went down. But he got up again, inspiring us all.

The wild diversity on RAGBRAI is missing one thing, though. I'm always disappointed when I notice the relatively narrow range of race and socioeconomic class represented on the ride. Most of us who participate on RAGBRAI are fairly well-off financially. It takes a comfortable income to afford this kind of vacation. Most of us are white. African Americans on RAGBRAI are rare. The *Des Moines Register*, however, has sponsored a racially mixed team of at-risk disadvantaged inner city kids from Des Moines for the last several years to train and ride together. They call themselves the Dream Team, and it's a great opportunity for the kids who sign on and complete the program. The sense of accomplishment that comes from riding their bikes across the state will stick with them for years. Maybe some day bicycling, like golf and tennis, will no longer be the recreational retreat of just affluent whites.

The great diversity of ability, machine, temperament, motivation, body-type, age, and clothing on RAGBRAI is a fitting illustration of what it is like to move through life with a disability. Just as the Iowa highways are tolerant of various types of clowns and rogues during this last week in July every year, society should be accommodating of those with disabilities. People with disabilities bring different gifts and perspectives to the table. All of life is enriched by their contributions.

But diversity on RAGBRAI isn't just a model for disability. It's a great metaphor for all of life. Isn't that how we all get through life? Tall or short, gay or straight, black or white, successful or goofy, we all traverse the same route from birth to death, each at our own pace and in our own manner. Some of us are gifted in certain areas, some in others. But we each play the same game. We do what we can to minimize our liabilities and maximize our assets. We play from our strengths. We rely on the gifts and passions we've been given, and note that others around us seem to rely on other strengths. We should revel in the diversity, make a party out of it, not demand conformity. Think of the fun we'd miss if we all did things the same way.

An illustration comes to mind. A few years ago there was a reality television program called "Junkyard Wars." In this show, two teams were placed in a large junkyard and their assignment was to build a sophisticated machine out of the parts they could scavenge. The team that built the most functional machine in the allotted time won. One week they built hill-climbing cars. Another week it was hovercraft. Once they had to build battering rams to bash through a brick wall. And then it was submarines. But in each episode of the show, all they had to use for materials was what they happened to find in the junkyard.

I submit that that's what each of us does to get through life. We each have at our disposal a smorgasbord of available resources. They include genetics, physical build, temperament, passions, emotional makeup, intelligence, habits, race, gender (and gender orientation), skills, gifts, experiences and training, and even weaknesses. We take this jumble of possibility and fashion out of it a life. It's like putting a puzzle together, except for the fact that you won't know what picture the puzzle makes until you've completed it. And you can put the pieces together in an infinite variety of ways, none of which is right or wrong. When you look at things from this perspective, it becomes clear that each individual is going to come up with a little different configuration. You may think, plan, organize, feel, and make decisions differently than I do. I'm going to excel in certain areas, and you're going to excel in others. How I worship and what I believe about God will be different from what you're comfortable with. We need to honor our differences, because that's how we were created.

Unfortunately, the current trend in our country is going in the opposite direction. There are more restrictions and more expectations of conformity. "English Only" and "Saving Marriage" are examples of how some in our society would pressure everyone else to fit in or get out. As if the fact that my neighbor speaks Spanish might somehow harm me, or as if the kid across the street with two dads or two moms might threaten the sanctity of my own marriage. If these things worry you, get a life. Find something more productive to worry about, like AIDS prevention in Africa or healthcare for all citizens in our country. On the contrary, I think these expressions of diversity only enrich the world we live in. We're entirely too parochial. The narrow image of physical beauty portrayed by magazine covers and movie stars forces impressionable young people into straitjackets of fashion and unhealthy eating patterns. We profile individuals with Arab-looking features because of our fear of terrorism. Diversity is not celebrated in contemporary culture; it is feared.

When my denomination, the United Church of Christ, gathers for its biennial national meeting, General Synod, it doesn't look like the church I'm accustomed to. My local church is a mostly white, mostly middle-to-upper-class, suburban, Midwestern, German-heritage congregation. And that's fine. They're good people. But when we gather on national and international levels, all colors, all races, all genders and gender orientations, many different cultures, and a wide range of abilities and disabilities are represented. The worship services look, feel, and sound nothing like my Sunday morning experiences. There's dancing, jazz, soul music, chant, many languages spoken and sung, strange liturgies. We don't always get out in an hour. The delegates who gather for these meetings don't all vote on moral and political and ecclesiastical issues the way my local congregation might vote. Wacky policies—at least they seem wacky to the good people out here in the Midwest—are endorsed.

But you know something? General Synod of the United Church of Christ is a richer expression of the life God calls us to than any merely local expression can ever be, just as RAGBRAI is a richer expression of bicycling than a lone cyclist on a city or country road can be. We each have our little piece of perspective on the truth, but our local expressions are always limited. We don't see the whole picture. We can't have the last word. No human expression can ever be definitive. But the more voices you get at the table, the closer you get. The raw diversity we experience when we gather together from many different places—which may make us uncomfortable and may seem challenging or even threatening—is God's gift. It reminds us that the world is bigger than our little corner of it.

The best biblical image of the kingdom of God in scriptures is in Luke's Gospel, chapter 12, where Jesus tells a parable of the great banquet. In this story, everyone gets invited just as they are. The blind, the lame, the crippled, the poor are all welcome at the feast. They aren't "normalized" first. They aren't all made to conform to society's standards. It's a come-as-you-are party.

I saw a glimpse of that kingdom just last week, reenacted in the neighborhood where my church is located. One of our neighbors, a white man of forty-four, had died. I'll call him Clyde. It's a poor inner-city neighborhood, and Clyde was not quite homeless but certainly marginal. He lived from welfare check to welfare check. He often came by the church's food pantry for assistance or hit up the secretaries in the office for a buck or two when he ran short.

But Clyde was a generous man, too, and as often as he came in need of assistance, he came to pay us back. Whenever he had a dollar or two to his name, he gave it to the church. Once he gave the office staff $20. Knowing him well, they kept the money in a drawer. Sure enough, a week later he came to borrow it back. Once when he received some sort of settlement check for a whopping $15,000, he offered to give that to the church, too. The church declined, but it seemed as though he had lots a friends for a while.

When he died I agreed to officiate at his funeral. Those who gathered, Clyde's "extended family," were a ragtag outfit. Clyde's brother, his next of kin and main contact, was fairly dysfunctional. A too-thin black man who was blind came. Clyde used to lead the blind man around the neighborhood by the hand. Now his brother was filling that role. Two black ladies showed up, a mother and daughter whom Clyde, a white man, had grown up with. Mother and daughter each had the same name. That must have been confusing at home. Clyde's fiancée of sixteen years came. The secretaries from my office came, bless their hearts, greeting the guests with sincerity and warmth. The volunteer director of our food pantry was there. And then the minister showed up—me—a crippled guy in a wheelchair. It was quite a circus. Our food pantry volunteer stood up at one point during the service and shared how Clyde had always wanted to give something back. One day, our food pantry volunteer had been struggling with the sign outside the church building, trying to put new lettering on the board in a cold, driving wind. Clyde had stopped by to see if he could help. He didn't need anything in return, just wanted to help. During the service, there was a little commotion as the blind neighbor found his way to the side of one of the church secretaries, whom he hit up for $5 "for a coke." She gave it to him.

Like RAGBRAI, this quirky little funeral beautifully illustrates my understanding of the kingdom of God. We're all a bunch of misfits and losers down here, flawed and limited human beings. We desperately cling to one another because we need help. We need others to watch out for us and lead us around the neighborhood. We need companions on our journey. We draft behind stronger riders. We sometimes need others to bring us pie or watermelon. But each one of us is also gifted in peculiar ways, and brings to the party a specialized set of gifts that in turn fill the needs of those around us.

We each get by using whatever gifts we may be able to muster, in whatever way we can. Differences are welcome. Another illustration of individual giftedness and adaptation comes from a story told about the famous violinist, Itzhak Perlman. I don't know if the story is true, but that doesn't matter. It's still a good story. One time Perlman came out on stage to begin a concert. A polio survivor, he walked across the stage with some difficulty, using clumsy leg braces and crutches. Once in place onstage, he had to unlock his braces, lean back into his chair, lay his crutches down, pick up his violin, and get ready to play. It was a laborious process. Unfortunately, immediately upon starting his piece of music, one of his violin strings broke.

The tension in the audience was almost tangible. What would he do? Would he have to put himself back together and walk offstage for a new violin? Would someone come to his rescue? How long would this take? We have a sitter at home, you know. Well, Perlman just sat there in silence for a moment, then he signaled the conductor to start the piece again. He played it through near flawlessly, tuning, adjusting, reconfiguring, almost recomposing the piece on the fly.

After the concert, Perlman was asked how he did it. His reply was, simply, "Sometimes it is the artist's task to make what music one can with what one has available."

That's the task of each one of us, not just the artist, not just the person with a disability, not just a cyclist rolling across the state of Iowa. We each get by doing our best with the materials at hand. How we determine to do it is a product of personal choice, not subject to legislation or judgment by the majority. My speed, my style, my version of the truth, my abilities or disabilities, my needs and my strengths all may be different from yours. But that's okay. Our individual foibles should be not only tolerated, but welcomed as gifts. We learn from one another through our differences. We should each ride a mile on each other's bicycle seat. As we pool our different strengths and perspectives, we come closer and closer to the feast of God's abundance.

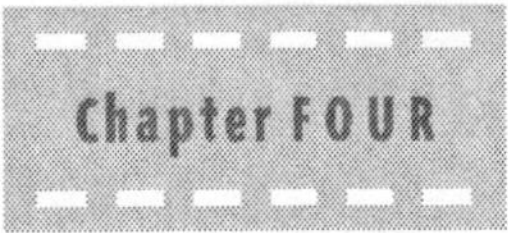

A Matter of Perspective

SAGGY THURSDAY is considered by common consensus to have been the second most grueling day's ride in all of RAGBRAI's history. We'll get to the number one worst day in the next chapter. It was 1995 and the route took cyclists from Tama to Sigourney. By late morning the heat had risen to intolerable levels and the wind, straight into our faces, was near gale force. We had to pedal hard down the hills just to keep from being blown back up them again. Strong riders were dropping like flies. Between one-third and one-half of all the cyclists "sagged" into Sigourney, hitching rides with whatever vehicles they could flag down.

I was among the stronger riders, yet I was having a time of it. I had ridden several miles during the morning slowly with my children and thus found myself out on the road later and under harsher conditions than I was accustomed to. It was brutal. I wasn't going to sag into Sigourney, so help me God, but I was clearly at the end of my endurance. Cyclists call it "bonking" or "hitting the wall." By the last dozen miles or so, I was needing any excuse to find shade, air conditioning, or a cold drink.

My friend and parishioner Porter French was supposed to have been on the ride that day. You remember old Porter. He's the one who volunteered to climb into the lovers' sleeping bag to quiet them down. We were supposed to meet outside of Belle Plaine. Porter, eighty-five years old at the time, was wearing his favorite tee shirt, which read, "Hello Matey, I'm over eighty."

I was seriously worried about him. Although he was a seasoned cyclist, these were no conditions for the aged or faint of heart. I was having enough trouble myself. I kept an eye out for Porter in the ditches, in case he had collapsed along the side of the road.

Then I spied him ahead. The rest of us were crouched down low over our handlebars, presenting a smaller target to the wind. Porter was sitting up ramrod straight on his big wide bike seat. He was pedaling as slow as was humanly possible and still remain upright. And there was a big smile on his face. I approached him incredulously, "Porter! How are you doing? Are you okay?"

"Oh, Bob," he said. "I'm fine."

"But the wind, the heat! How do you survive this?"

"I'm having a great day," he maintained. "At the speed I ride the wind is hardly a factor. And this heat is great. I haven't had to pee all day."

Instead of hunkering down and fighting a duel to the death with the elements, Porter just accepted things as they were and made the best of them, thereby providing a model for the rest of us in dealing not only with RAGBRAI conditions, but with all the adverse conditions that life throws at us. Adjusting to disability is like that. Dealing with rush hour traffic is like that. Having a good day is more about a decision you make when you get up in the morning than it is about what happens to you during the day.

Once I was invited to speak to a building full of middle-school students on "Accentuate the Positive" day. Talk about a challenging assignment! Have you ever faced an auditorium full of squirming seventh-graders? They can be intimidating. Anyway, I started out by asking the group for a show of hands: Who among them was having a good day? Then I asked who was having a bad day. The responses were about evenly divided. Then I went on to ask those who had reported a bad day what happened today to make it a bad day. I got a whole range of answers, from a broken pencil to a broken arm, from a bad grade to a bad relationship. But as we got more deeply into the discussion, it became apparent that some of the students who were having a good day were having more terrible things happen to them than some of the students having a bad day. In fact, there was a freshly broken arm in the good day group. She said it gave her an excuse to get out of school. There was also a broken relationship in the good day group. He was glad to be rid of her. In short, you can never assume from external occurrences whether an experience will be good or bad. It's an internal thing. It has to do with temperament or decision or will, not with circumstance.

Being stuck in rush hour traffic can seem like a tragedy if you're late for a meeting. But it can also feel like a blessing. Maybe you didn't want to go to that meeting anyway. It can be a blessing if, in the middle of a busy day, you get stuck in traffic and there's nothing you can do about it, so you listen to soothing music and breathe deeply. You accept the delay as a gift from God.

The late Henri J. M. Nouwen, whom I studied under at Yale Divinity School, was a prolific writer in the field of Christian spirituality. He would agree that joy in life is more a matter a choice than it is a result of circumstances.

> We do have a choice, not so much in regard to the circumstances of our life, but in regard to the way we respond to these circumstances. Two people can be the victims of the same accident. For the one, it becomes the source of resentment; for the other, the source of gratitude. The external circumstances are the same, but the choice of response is completely different. Some people grow bitter as they grow old. Others grow old joyfully. That does not mean that the life of those who become bitter was harder than the life of those who become joyful. It means that different choices were made, inner choices, choices of the heart.[20]

Nouwen says, "Choose joy." He talks about a friend of his who "radiates joy, not because his life is easy, but because he habitually recognizes God's presence in the midst of all human suffering."

> Whenever I meet him, I am tempted to draw his attention to the wars between nations, the starvation among children, the corruption in politics, and the deceit among people, thus trying to impress him with the ultimate brokenness of the human race. But every time I try something like this, he looks at me with his gentle and compassionate eyes and says: "I saw two children sharing their bread with one another, and I heard a woman say 'thank you' and smile when someone covered her with a blanket. These simple poor people gave me new courage to live my life."[21]

I use a wheelchair to get around. A casual observer might conclude that's a tragedy. A man in his prime, forced to live as an invalid (the observer's word, not mine). Assumptions are made, by people who don't know me, about what my life must be like, how difficult it must be, what I must have given up in order to continue living. I know this is true because I've made the same sort of assumptions about others. I still make them, in fact, when I should know better. The wheelchair is, after all, the most visible external circumstance of my life.

But assumptions about my level of joy and the personal satisfaction I may or may not continue to derive from life would be premature. Because those things don't depend on circumstances; they depend on decision. I decided to get back into the game of life, wheelchair or not. It's true that there are moments of deep frustration and anguish. I feel grief and loss often. Like the day of the bike ride into Sigourney, there's no denying the difficulty. But how we respond to that is up to us. I choose to choose joy, rather than frustration. It can be done.

Some people would argue that we can change the circumstance side of the equation. If we pray hard enough or believe strongly enough in God's supernatural power, then we can remove whatever obstacles are in our way. Expect a miracle. Faith can move mountains, the Bible says.

Many people have urged me toward that position. Indeed, it almost seemed natural. One of my favorite parishioners came up to me on my first Sunday back at church following my accident and said to me, "Bob, if anyone can walk again after an accident like yours, it would be you. I just know that your faith is strong enough to get you on your feet again." It seemed like the right thing to say. I once rolled into a church service in another city and was immediately greeted by a stranger who wanted to know if she could pray for me. She grasped my hands and proceeded to petition her Lord to drive out the demons from my heart that kept me in this wheelchair. She pleaded that I be restored to health (I didn't feel it was my place to inform her that I was already enjoying perfect health) and that strength be renewed in my legs. Nothing happened. Should I assume she was a woman of little faith? Or did my cynicism jinx her spell—I mean her prayer? I tell people I've already received my miracle. I'm alive and have been led back into the life I loved before my injury. I am a whole human being in spite of my disability. It would be greedy of me to demand another miracle. I'd certainly accept it if offered, but I'm not putting my life on hold waiting for it.

I counseled once with a man who was suffering from a degenerative neurological disease that had deprived him of the use of his legs. He was in a wheelchair now, and in tears. "I have prayed for healing," he said. "My church has prayed for me. I've been to healing services. Godly pastors have laid hands on me. I've even been exorcised. But nothing works, and I'm getting worse. The Bible says if you have faith like a mustard seed, you can move mountains. I can't even move my toes anymore. What's wrong with me?"

This poor man was crippled not only by his disease, but by his theology. His faith was a handicap to his acceptance of the circumstances of his life and spiritual growth. I don't believe prayer is going to fix everything that's broken in our world.

The world was created flawed and we have to learn to live within it. God's role is to help us pick up the pieces.

My experience and my observations of the experiences of others would lead me to believe that the circumstances of my life and the world around me do not respond directly to my petitions. If they did, I would see to it that innocent people would never die in plane crashes or that cancer might never afflict good, loving people. I'd also pray for flat, tail wind days on RAGBRAI. How does 72 degrees sound? Or would you like it a tad warmer? But God doesn't seem to respond to this kind of prayer. In spite of countless prayers on behalf of innocent victims, tragic things still happen. For whatever reason—and that's another book—bad things happen to good people.[22] Recognizing this basic fact of life does not limit God, it's just being honest. The biblical image of God never included omnipotence. That doctrine has been added over the centuries. We don't control what happens to us. All we can control is our response to what happens. If we want to be joyful people, we can't afford to wait until the planets align and our ship comes in.

Nouwen, again, says:

> Joy does not come from positive predictions about the state of the world. It does not depend on the ups and downs of the circumstances of our lives. Joy is based on the spiritual knowledge that, while the world in which we live is shrouded in darkness, God has overcome the world. Jesus says it loudly and clearly: "In the world you will have troubles, but rejoice, I have overcome the world."[23]

When our son, Ames, was just five years old, he was diagnosed with leukemia. The weekend of the diagnosis tore our hearts apart. He'd been experiencing pain in his foot and I'd had to carry him around on my back for a couple of days, so we decided it was high time for him to see his pediatrician. Maybe there was a sprain or fracture. Ann took him to the doctor on a Friday.

She called me from the doctor's office and told me they had to see him at University Hospital, and that I should meet them there. My heart just sank. In a little consulting room, the resident dropped the word *cancer* like a little time bomb. It sat there in the room between us like a menacing thing; we waited, stunned, to see if it would go off. They told us to take Ames home for the weekend and then admit him in the hospital first thing Monday morning. We felt almost like it was a weekend reprieve before the death sentence could be commuted. There was no hope in our hearts, just a heavy burden. Our world was black.

But on the way home, along some of the same rural highways that RAGBRAI had followed (and would follow again), we saw in the sky the most amazing sign. It was dark and cloudy, but all of a sudden the sun punched through the clouds to the west, and there in the east was one of the brightest rainbows we had ever seen. Set off against the darkness of its background, it looked luminous, like it had been painted on the threatening sky with neon colors. We were so stunned we pulled off onto the shoulder, stopped the car, and got out to hug one another under this sign of promise. God would be with us through this. It would be okay.

Almost exactly eleven years later, my wife was sitting in a hospital emergency waiting room. She had been there for three days while the trauma surgeons operated on me and tried to pull me back from beyond the brink of death. But that night she woke up with a vision. It would be okay, she had been assured. There was no certainty about the outcome. I might live or I still might die. We can never be certain about outcomes and circumstances. But she had been assured, in some mystical way, that God would be with her and me and our family through this ordeal, and that it would be okay.

I've found that living with a permanent disability often calls for a Zen-like patience. It can be downright frustrating to be in a wheelchair. There are moments I want to scream. Every social gathering becomes an obstacle course. From where I sit, I'm not visible to the crowd. I went to see Lance Armstrong and hear him speak in Coralville last summer on RAGBRAI. Got there early and took my place in the middle of the sweltering parking lot. But by the time The Man took the stage I was so completely engulfed in a sea of people who, standing, were two feet taller than I am in my chair that I couldn't see or hear a thing. I might as well have stayed home.

I can't maneuver through a crowded room. I can't get to the buffet table when the tables and chairs are placed too close together. It's an effort to get into and out of my car, and, fit as I am, sometimes I'm just not up to the ongoing challenge. I'm sometimes weary of the exacting care and planning that goes into each day so that I don't end up stranded somehow during the day. Once in a while, for example, I'll be driving with a passenger in my car, and then drop that person off at their destination. It may not have occurred to either of us, unless I'm constantly vigilant, that my wheelchair is still in the back end of my car. And I have no way to get at it or get out of my car without it. I have to drive around town until I spot a passerby who responds to my request for help. I can't even phone for help, since my phone is in my chair.

I shared with a group recently that there is one circumstance in which I really resent having a disability. Actually, there are two circumstances, but this was a mixed audience with some minors present, and I didn't think talking about sexual performance was exactly appropriate. You understand.

I'm a serious athlete, wheelchair or not. I train rigorously and systematically throughout the year for wheelchair marathons, triathlons, and handcycle events like RAGBRAI. In regional handcycle competitions drawing from all over the Midwest I have consistently placed in the top three, so I'm no slouch. But the moments I just hate are when I'm on RAGBRAI, cranking up a hill to the fullest extent of my ability. Handcycles don't go uphill very fast. They're heavy and there's no way one's arms are going to get as strong as a good set of legs. We're at a definite disadvantage, relative to a normal two-wheel cycle, on the hills. So I'm climbing a hill, cranking as hard as I can, when I hear this "*ka-ching*" behind me. It's a little girl on a pink one-speed Schwinn with colorful handlebar streamers and a wicker basket. She has one of those little tin bells mounted on the handlebar. She rings the damn thing again as she passes me going up the hill. "You're doing great, mister!" she calls out as she breezes by, her pigtails bouncing in the breeze. Moments like these, I resent my disability with all my heart. I'm thinking "You ring that bell one more time and I'm going to stuff it down your throat." But I say out loud, between rasping breaths, "Thanks sweetie, you're looking good yourself." Ministers have the art of diplomacy deeply ingrained.

Challenges such as these are a given for someone living with a disability. They're not going to go away. Several times a day—maybe several times an hour—we feel like we've been cut off in traffic. The rest of the world is moving right along while we're stuck in the slow lane. When those things happen, I have a choice to make. On the one hand, I can lament my lot in life, sit back hoping and praying for a miracle cure to remove me from these troubling circumstances, and rail with anger against the injustice of it all. I admit, sometimes I take this course. But, like I say, it's a choice. In my more lucid moments, I am able to accept, even embrace, these circumstances. Everybody has something to deal with. We all face limitations and challenges. These happen to be mine. They're distracting, but they're manageable. I began my previous book by reflecting, "It was not what I would have chosen for my life. But I have, over the last five years, *decided* to choose it. And that has made all the difference."[24]

What Porter had going for him that day on RAGBRAI was that he was riding in the present, in the here-and-now. He had no preconceived notions about how fast he should be going or what time he should be expected to arrive at the next town. He bailed out after a few miles, calling his wife to come pick him up, so that he wouldn't threaten his health. He was in the ride for the long haul, you see.

Porter died the very next year, at the local hospital. No, he wasn't a patient at the hospital. He was serving as volunteer chaplain. He was something of a gadfly to the administrators of the hospital, insisting that the patients have spiritual as well as physical care. He was making photocopies of a prayer he had written for patients in distress when he keeled over from a massive heart attack. One thing you can say for Porter: he lived until he died.

But while Porter, bless his soul, was enjoying Saggy Thursday for what it offered, I was constantly monitoring my onboard computer, increasingly dismayed at my slowing average speed. My friend Austin recently got a heart monitor and a GPS tracking computer so he can instantly measure energy output, average speed, elapsed and remaining time and distance, and several other important readings, and later plot the whole thing on a computer printout so that he can program training routines designed to improve on his performance under similar circumstances in the future. He emails me his readings so we can monitor the rides together. I have another biking buddy who refuses to use a cycling computer, knowing how it will change his perspective. When he uses a computer, he becomes obsessive over speed, just like Austin and I tend to do. Without a computer, he finds he rides more like Porter, who was just finding enjoyment in the day. Which is the best way to approach the town of Sigourney on a day like Saggy Thursday? Or on any day?

Nouwen says we would all benefit from being able to be truly attentive to the present moment, although he recognizes the difficulties involved.

> It is hard to live in the present. The past and the future keep harassing us. The past with guilt, the future with worries. So many things have happened in our lives about which we feel uneasy, regretful, angry, confused, or, at least, ambivalent. And these feelings are often colored by guilt. . . .
>
> Worse, however, than our guilt are our worries. Our worries fill our lives with "What ifs". . .
>
> To live in the present, we must believe deeply that what is most important is the here and the now. We are

> constantly distracted by things that have happened in the past or that might happen in the future. It is not easy to remain focused on the present. Our mind is hard to master and keeps pulling us away from the moment.[25]

So how do we go about doing that, focusing our minds on the pleasure of the present moment without being distracted by past regrets or future worries? We'll spend a little time talking about helpful disciplines in a later chapter. Nouwen recommends prayer to center on what is the most important in our lives. In prayer we can filter out the distractions and be truly present to the moment at hand. Essential Christian prayer is not just asking God for things, the way most people imagine. Prayer is an attempt to be open to the gift of the present moment.

There are days on RAGBRAI when the topic of conversation swirls around an upcoming challenging hill. The Pilot Mound Hill outside Ames, for example, strikes dread into the hearts of seasoned cyclists. When the route takes us up the Pilot Mound Hill, that's all people can seem to talk about. "Save something for the hill!" "Better eat an extra pork burger for breakfast today. We've got the Pilot Mound Hill to contend with." RAGBRAI novices wonder, "Will I be able to make it up the Pilot Mound Hill?" Nouwen would call that worrying about the future. But, truth be told, if you somehow missed the memo about the Big Hill on today's route, you'd get there, climb it, and be on your way without a second thought. You might not even notice it. Hills have a way of flattening themselves out when you don't make a big deal of them.

I wish I had a more attentive attitude. Most people around me are far better at being attentive to the present than I am. I always have an agenda. Even when I'm talking with someone about something else, I'm always plotting two or three moves ahead. My parishioners may think I'm listening attentively to them when I'm really planning the agenda for an upcoming meeting or making out a grocery list in my head. I'm not bragging. I know that's not a good thing. But that's my temperament. I'm always on my way somewhere. I'm always trying to arrive. For me, distractions become obstacles, not gifts. The heat, head winds, and hills were all distractions that day, interfering with my goal of arriving in Sigourney. I'm not sure why I was so keen on arriving in Sigourney, except for the fact that arrival would signal the end to this torture out on the road, but that was my single-minded focus for the day. Porter, on the other hand, got it. He managed to find pleasure in the moment.

It doesn't help to try not to worry about things like the heat and hills and slow speeds. That turns into an exercise of futility, like trying *not* to think of an elephant. Have you ever tried *not* to think of an elephant? What's the first thing that pops into your head when you try *not* to think of an elephant? An elephant. It's impossible, and your failure becomes just one more source of worry and bother.

What may work better, perhaps, for some people, is to think about something bigger than their immediate problems. A big worry can cancel out the small ones. Focusing on the bigger picture can put into perspective the petty concerns that are bothering us at the moment. In the big scheme of things, just how important is this one day of cycling, anyway? I mean, for goodness sake. People are dying of starvation and AIDS, wars are being waged, politicians are making decisions to cut benefits from millions of poor people so that the wealthy can squirrel away another million dollars a year. And we're out here cycling from one Iowa town to the next. Let's keep things in perspective. One year I slapped a "U.S. out of El Salvador" bumper sticker on the kids' trailer that I pulled behind my bike, as my little attempt to place the ride on a higher moral plane. Another year I had organized a fundraising and speaking tour along the RAGBRAI route for the director of our United Church of Christ Hunger Action office, though he ultimately had to cancel due to scheduling conflicts. This past year I wore a United Church of Christ jersey and tried to gather up those who noticed the shirt and claimed UCC affiliation into a group for a photo op later in the week. It helps to have something other than discomfort to focus on.

Often our problem is that we are attempting to break life down into specific problems to tackle. The scientific method breaks the world down into manageable components that can be observed, analyzed, quantified, and, therefore, "understood." My tendency on the Sigourney road was to break the miles down into distances that could be covered. As I measured the time it took to cover those distances, my outlook got increasingly gloomier. Porter approached the day from a different paradigm. He took the day as a whole and simply accepted and lived within it.

Matthew Fox talks about life not as a problem to be solved, but a mystery before which we should simply stand in awe. Our Western mindset tempts us to try to control the elements, to manipulate the environment. Fox, in line with Christian and Eastern mysticism, argues that we are more true to who we were created to be when we simply marvel at the wonder around us. Taking life as mystery is also a better strategy for living.

> The French philosopher and art critic Gabriel Marcel suggests that we postindustrial adults become so programmed to solving problems that we lose our capacity to wonder and become ecstatic at mysteries. A problem (from the Greek *proballo*, meaning to throw in front of) is an object. Like a tree fallen across a road [or a headwind on a hot day into Sigourney] it is outside of me, an obstruction, and may be resolved by removal or rearrangement. "A problem is something met with which bars my passage. It is before me in its entirety." A mystery, on the other hand, is something in which I find myself caught up and whose essence is therefore not to be before me in its entirety. A mystery is decidedly not an unsolvable problem that needs rearrangement or removal to be resolved. Marcel warns that we are engaged in a "fundamentally vicious proceeding" when we, whether as individuals or as a culture, "reduce a mystery to a problem."[26]

So one way to react to difficulty in life is to accept it as part of the mystery of the matrix of living, as Porter seems to have been able to do. Take the good and the bad, and give thanks for the whole lot.

But there's another sort of discipline that helps many people get through difficult times. I have a very thoughtful friend, Greg, who rides RAGBRAI as often as he can. Greg is the former director of the Iowa Peace Institute. The Institute has now ceased to exist, although it has morphed into a peace studies center at Grinnell College. Most every year following RAGBRAI, Greg comes up with a lesson that he has learned during the ride, and he shares these things with me. Greg is responsible, for example, for the reflection in chapter six that the snacks are always at the top of the hill.

This past year, Greg emailed me with his latest life lesson from RAGBRAI. "Just pedal circles," was all he had to say. When I emailed him back to ask him to flesh out this reflection a bit, he simply said that "just pedal circles" became his mantra this year. It helped him climb the hills and not get discouraged.

Pedaling circles is a concept used by elite racers to fine-tune their pedaling strokes. You might not expect there to be much technique in pushing bicycle pedals, but there is. Novices trying to get power out of the bike tend to mash big gears and just hammer up and down. This is known as "pedaling squares." By pumping your legs up and down like pistons, you're actually squandering energy and working against the circular shape of the motion of the cranks. Lance Armstrong is renowned in racing circles for his smooth pedaling stroke. He was able to exert power along every inch of the circumference of the path of his pedals. He had perfected pedaling in circles.

It's also a psychological concept, or at least it is for Greg. People may have wondered why this sixty-something bearded gent was muttering "justpedalcircles-justpedalcircles-justpedalcircles-justpedalcircles" as he slowly inched past them up inclines, but the truth is, his mantra got him to the top. It helped him focus on the next steps, baby steps, instead of worrying over the entire climb. It was his way of being in the present moment.

An example of the pedal-circles mentality occurred on the ride in 1974, RAGBRAI's second year. Political historians will recognize 1974 as a watershed year in American politics, and the first week in August as a particularly significant week. It was during the Watergate hearings. Everything came to a head that week, as President Richard Nixon was becoming more and more embattled. Finally he announced his resignation in order to avoid impeachment. Donald Kaul's newspaper column from RAGBRAI that day read, "The general reaction of the riders was, 'How much farther to Guthrie Center?' When you're out on the open road with the cattle lowing . . . the problems of Richard (the President) Nixon seem very far away, indeed."[27] While the world was spinning around them, two thousand riders were focusing on the task at hand. Just pedaling circles.

That's what RAGBRAI does to a rider. That's why people like to do it. All politics, all career pressures, even family issues are swept out of your mind as you contemplate the two basic essentials: getting to the next town and finding some food. It's the perfect vacation because it really is impossible to take your work with you. People focus small on RAGBRAI. They just pedal circles.

Many people are stalked by depression because they can't pedal circles. They can't get the big picture out of their heads. They worry about possible outcomes, what can go wrong, the pressures that build up. Often the only way out of the abyss of concern is to begin to break down the problems to the immediate. What can I do this day, this hour, even this minute? Take baby steps. Just pedal circles.

In fact, now that I think of it, pedaling circles is how I was able to recover to the extent that I have from my injury. The job ahead for the physical therapy staff was monumental. They had to whip me back into shape as a professional pastor and engaged father and competitive athlete from the near-vegetative state in which they found me. I'm sure they never looked that far ahead. In their wisdom, the physical therapists kept incremental tasks ahead of me. I learned to sit up. Speak. Roll over. Good dog. They threw me treats at the end of particularly strenuous days.

I learned to transfer into my wheelchair and push it independently. I got stronger and learned to drive with hand controls. Each little task of daily living was an accomplishment. If I had sat and contemplated how far I would have to come, and how difficult each step was to be, I never would have gotten out of bed that first day of therapy.

I pedal circles in my professional life. A major project in the church is undertaken by breaking it down into its component steps and determining at each stage who will do what, how it will be done, and by when. Through no fault or virtue of my own, I was gifted with a personality type that helps me see both the forest and the trees. That's what successful managers do. They have an uncanny ability to break the massive down into its incremental parts and then tackle one at a time, monitoring the whole process.

Jesus had the answer to the problems we encountered on the road to Sigourney. And it wasn't to show up and calm the winds like he did for his friends adrift on the Sea of Galilee (although many of us were praying for just such a visitation that afternoon). A better solution for us was when he said, "Don't fret about what you will eat or drink or what you will wear or how you will make a living. Don't worry about being the first cyclist to the next town." I'm paraphrasing here. "The town will still be there when you arrive. Don't worry about the weather. If it rains you'll get wet. If it's hot, you'll get hot. You can bank on it. Don't worry that your bike isn't as expensive as that of the kid who just passed you. Don't mind that the little girl on the pink Schwinn is faster than you are. Don't sweat the small stuff. But focus instead on the big picture. Are you happy to be here? Having a good time? Does it beat working? This day is a free gift from me to you. Enjoy it. Be grateful. Quit your bellyaching. Set your mind on God's Kingdom, an expression of compassion and harmony for all, and you'll get to where you're going in the end. Or you won't, but that will be okay, too." Too often we get bogged down in the details, forgetting what's really valuable.

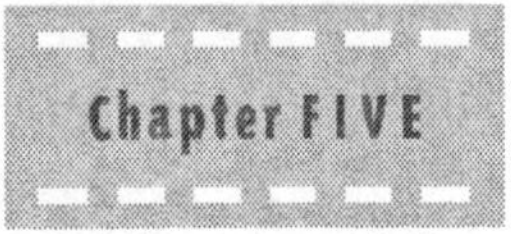

Chapter FIVE

We Get By with a Little Help from Our Friends

BACK IN the old days before my injury, when I could ride strongly away from the front of the pack, I imagined myself to be in control of my experience and strong enough that I didn't need any help from anyone. I could fill up my water bottles, stuff a couple of bananas in my jersey pockets, and be entirely self-sufficient for three or four hours of hard riding—more than enough for a sixty- to eighty-mile ride.

The bananas in the pockets remind me of my best RAGBRAI story ever. It doesn't relate to the theme of this chapter—it doesn't relate to any of my themes—but it's too good to leave out. I used to ride with a friend, Tom, who was even a stronger rider than I. He'd stick his banana in the back of the waistband of his shorts and ride nonstop for hours. Tom was a gregarious, chatty fellow. One time we rode past two elderly couples riding together. The ladies were riding just ahead of the men. We passed the men first, said hello, and then caught up to the ladies. Tom called to them, "Are you two attractive young ladies riding with those old geezers back there? How 'bout riding with us for awhile?" Without missing a beat, one of them replied, "Those old geezers have more in the *front* of their pants than you have in the *back* of yours."

Well, enough of that. Back to the topic at hand. We subscribe to the Great American Myth of the loner cowboy, tall in the saddle, independent and determined. We still buy into it on many different levels. But my return to RAGBRAI by handcycle has taught me that we all rely on the kindness of strangers to get us by. In my previous book I shared a story about getting help along the road when I had a flat tire. I had patches and a pump, but nothing I did seemed to work. The tire kept going flat. By the time the adventure was resolved, an ad hoc army of a couple dozen people had helped me get to the next little town, Roland, and Roland's mayor had fetched me a cold beer from his icebox.

Stories like that abound. This year I encountered a quadriplegic handcyclist. Quads face more daunting circumstances than paraplegics, as you might imagine. Being quadriplegic doesn't mean a person has no movement in any of their limbs. It just means that all four limbs are affected to some degree. This guy with no use of his legs and limited upper body strength was out on RAGBRAI, riding a handcycle similar to mine. But he had a unique add-on. Mounted vertically on the back of his cycle was a sturdy staff, about the size and length of a baseball bat. On top of the staff was posted a little sign that read, plaintively, "Help. Please push me." As he would begin ascending a hill, able-bodied riders going by would see the sign and push him up the hill. He claimed that in the 444 miles across the state of Iowa this past summer, he had only had to crank up one hill by himself. I may try that next year. In fact, I'll go one better. I'll put a little sign on the back of my bike that reads, "Help. Please push me. And give me a dollar." If it works, I'll make ten grand on the trip!

Just outside of the little town of Cosgrove this past summer, the RAGBRAI route turned north and slammed unexpectedly into a short hill that was bordering on vertical. "Mount Cosgrove" they're already calling it. It will go down in the annals of RAGBRAI legend. Encountering that hill was one of those rude and surprising moments when a rider is knocked from his or her highest gear down to the lowest gear—if you were lucky enough to have seen the hill coming and managed to make the downshift—and it still isn't low enough. It was hot, we were unprepared for the all-out demands of the hill, and it just didn't seem fair somehow. Why was God punishing us? I know it seems silly now to think that our Supreme Creator and Ruler of the Universe would have nothing better to do with Her time than to throw obstacles in the path of a clump of vacationing bicycle riders in Iowa, but that's how it seemed to us at the moment. The human mind wants excuses. We want to know why Bad Things happen. This hill looked like a Bad Thing. To add insult to injury, upon cresting that hill, riders discovered that there were two or three more just like it before arriving at Cosgrove. By the time I dragged myself into town, my arms were cramping and I wasn't sure I could do even one more of those hills the rest of the day.

But Cosgrove was not ADA compliant (ADA is the Americans with Disabilities Act of 1990, which helped level the playing field for persons with disabilities). I sat for a time in the middle of a parking lot, heat radiating off my drenched jersey and overheated helmet, realizing I couldn't get through the throngs of cyclists into the air-conditioned oasis of the community building for pie and lemonade. Remember, once I get on my handcycle in the morning and put my wheelchair on the charter truck to be delivered at the next overnight town, I'm stuck in my cycle. I can't get off it to go through a food line or get into a bathroom. It's just one of those occupational hazards that takes some logistical creativity. I was trapped in the parking lot. And I was in no shape to continue the ride into the next town, several more hills away.

I needed a hug.

And then, amazingly, that was exactly what I got. Sort of. The ladies in the community building selling pie noticed my plight. They came bustling out and made a path for me to the community building. They threw open the doors. Making a big fuss, they pulled me into the cool, dark building, shooed some riders away from a table so I could wheel up to it ("You boys get away from there. This man needs a place at the table. Go on, get!"), and they brought me a big slab of peach pie, a bottle of water, and a big glass of lemonade. Hospitality never tasted so good. I needed help, and help arrived. We often don't know what support is out there until we let down our guard and show our vulnerability.

One year the ride followed a recreational trail from Waterloo to Cedar Rapids. There were hundreds of riders who took that optional trail in order to see a different part of the state. Right next to the trail was a pie and coffee shop in a little town. Naturally, hundreds of cyclists stopped for refreshment.

Now I don't know if that little shop didn't get the memo that RAGBRAI was coming through, or if the proprietor didn't realize that her shop was the only food stand for fifty miles, but they were not equipped for several hundred riders. The place only seated thirty or forty. It seemed they had enough pie on hand, but there was only one very harried little old lady waiting tables. It simply wouldn't do.

By the time I got there with some friends and found a place to sit, the frustration level was building. Then one brave soul did what was needed. He got up and poured himself a cup of coffee. Then he refilled some other cups at his table. And then some other cups around the restaurant. Then, when the carafe went dry, he went to the machine and made some more. Then people started getting up and cutting themselves wedges of pie and serving each other from behind the counter. Everyone was finally getting fed. It was a loaves and fishes miracle. Maybe that's really how it really happened in Jesus' day. As a miracle story the loaves and fishes tale makes good reading, but in reality people may just have started breaking out what bread and fish they had with them and sharing it. It has a bit more pizzazz the way it's written, but this interpretation makes it all about hospitality and helping one's neighbors.

It would be fair to wonder about what went on at that coffee shop: Were we stealing the food? Not at all. Everyone who ate and drank left money. Most left more than the price listed on the wall. And another bike rider got up and started collecting all the money that was left on the tables and deposited it in the cash register. I have no way of knowing, but it seems to me that little old lady could have retired to Sun City after the windfall she made that day. People help each other out on RAGBRAI in ways that they never do in real life. There are countless stories of purses or wallets that are left behind at food stands that miraculously find their way back to their rightful owners. Farmers leave their fields to drive exhausted riders into town. Homes are opened up to house the weary. RAGBRAI comes very close to resembling the biblical image of the Kingdom of God, where the hungry are fed, the poor are given good things, the blind and the lame are accommodated at the table of blessing.

"Soggy Monday" is widely regarded by the RAGBRAI community as the worst day in the history of the ride. I wasn't on board that year, but everybody who is familiar with RAGBRAI knows about it. It was the second day of the ride in 1981. The first day of the ride had been cold and drizzly. The second day, Soggy Monday, was a day from hell. The high temperature was only 52 degrees. It hovered in the 40s most of the day. For July in Iowa, that was absolutely frigid. It rained buckets all day. And there was a stiff head wind against the riders clocked at 35 miles per hour. Hypothermia was a real danger. The plague of riders, like locusts on a grain field, stripped clothing stores along the route clean of anything warm for sale. They were buying suits and bathrobes, tuxes and overalls. It didn't matter what size they were, as long as the cyclists could bundle up for awhile in something dry and warm. Riders were bailing out all day. Karras tells a touching story of a local farmer who rose to the occasion.

> Donald Meyer who farms near Schleswig transported bikers free. He packed his horse trailer and two other vehicles driven by his wife and daughter with bikes and bikers and refused to take a cent. "Look," he told one of the cyclists, "three weeks ago my beans and corn were an absolute disaster. The good Lord gave me this rain yesterday and today that saved my crops and the least I can do in thanks is to help out with some of these six thousand people who've been inconvenienced by the rain that

> saved the whole thing that I've got invested." The people he saved kept pressing money on him and he finally agreed to take it and give it to his church.[28]

Why can't we live that way the rest of the year? Why can't we do nice things for one another, take care of sisters and brothers in need, and graciously receive help when we are vulnerable? Why can't we vote that way, so that our political arrangements reflect these values? Maybe we just get tired and selfish. And I think our cultural myths get in the way.

In our culture we often fool ourselves by thinking that we have pulled ourselves up by our own bootstraps and that therefore everybody else should do the same. I wish I had a nickel for every time I've heard my father-in-law, a retired military officer, conservative, dyed-in-the-wool Republican, say that. I could retire and not have to supplement my pastor's salary by writing books. Anybody who isn't succeeding must not be trying hard enough. Their own deficiencies are keeping them down. We think of ourselves as self-sufficient cowboys and we tend to be critical of those who can't "make it" on their own. "Get your own health insurance. I got mine." Our health system is scandalous in the way that it abandons the poor. Cyclists crossing Iowa would never leave an injured bicyclist behind on the side of the road, but that's the way our healthcare system operates.

This take-care-of-yourself view ignores the systemic nature of social and political barriers, and overlooks the invisible networks of relationships that provide some people with advantages while leaving others behind. Talk about invisible subsidies: The taxpayers of the city where I now live just paid the Wal-Mart Corporation nineteen million dollars for the privilege of allowing it to erect one of its stores across the street from my house, so that the Walton family and its company's shareholders could get even richer by paying workers wages so low they would still need to apply for public assistance to have enough to get by. Our tax dollars are hard at work subsidizing the already-obscenely wealthy to both build and employ. It's quite a gig, if you can get it. So much for free-market competition. I don't mind sharing wealth so that the poor might live—the common good is something we should all aspire toward and pay for—but giving the Wal-Mart Corporation tax incentives is a little like Lance Armstrong getting a push up a hill by a quadriplegic cyclist.

Marcus Borg writes:

> Our culture's ethos of individualism generates a political ideology benefiting elites in particular. It legitimates their place in society: if you have prospered, it's because you have worked hard and made good use of your opportunities; you deserve what you've got. It legitimates social and economic policies that increase private wealth and generate public poverty. It legitimates blaming the poor. The conclusion strikes me as compelling: we have an elite-driven social and economic policy.[29]

A faith that emphasizes individual spirituality at the expense of social justice tends to legitimate the status quo, leaving in place oppressive social structures that reward the few at the expense of the many. In our country, 1 percent of the population controls 43 percent of the wealth. While a tiny minority is making obscenely big bucks, the median family income is just $28,000 a year. What is the practical impact of this great class divide? One very prominent example comes quickly to mind. Those who were unable to evacuate from New Orleans and the Gulf Coast before, during, and after Hurricane Katrina in 2005 were overwhelmingly poor, elderly, and black residents of the region. The tragedy that resulted was a clear indication that huge numbers of vulnerable people do not share in the resources of society that many of us take for granted—in this case a resource as simple as transportation out of a zone that is facing clear and immediate danger. These people were, quite literally, left behind. Our society turned a callous eye toward their plight, and incredibly, in some instances, blamed the victims for their own suffering.

Borg continues:

> The dream of God has been submerged by the individualism that characterizes much of modern Western culture. The dream of God is quite different from contemporary American dreams. The dream of God—a politics of compassion and justice, the kingdom of God, a domination-free order—is social, communal, and egalitarian. But our dreams—the dreams we get from our culture—are individualistic: living well, looking good, standing out.[30]

Borg asks his students to try to discern American conventional wisdom and then come up with popular phrases that express that understanding. Consistently, they call up the slogans of rugged individualism that characterize our times:

> Be all you can be.
> Just do it.
> Whoever dies with the most toys wins.
> You only go around once.
> Go for the gusto.
> Look out for number one.
> You deserve a break today.
> You're worth it.
> Nice guys finish last.
> Membership has its privileges.

There are few popular messages emerging out of our culture that reflect a passion for building a just society, working for the common good, or compassion toward others. This individualism is deeply ingrained. Robert Bellah, in *Habits of the Heart: Individualism and Commitment in American Life*, the now-classic study first published in 1985, observed that individualism has become the central strand of American life. It permeates every aspect of culture, from politics and work to family life and even religion. Personal fulfillment has become our goal.

A most insidious expression of this individualism infects even religious beliefs. Popular religion (the stuff I get sucked into on TV when I'm channel surfing and there's nothing else on) consistently calls people to individualistic expressions of faith. There's little mention of the prophetic thread that runs through both Old and New Testaments of the Bible. The prophets called their societies to account for neglecting the welfare of the widow, the orphan, and the sojourner—the ones who had no political rights. Socially, politically, and ecclesiastically these outsiders were considered expendable, disposable. But prophetic faith regarded them as valuable children of God. Prophets would measure the success of a king's reign by how well he had treated the poor.

Jesus placed himself squarely in the prophetic lineage, preaching not just individual salvation but offering a vision of a just and egalitarian community. His ministry was most clearly identified by how he reached across social barriers to welcome outsiders. He openly spoke with women. He consorted and ate with tax collectors. He touched and healed the sick. Back in his time, a rabbi or holy person would have been rendered unclean by contact with a diseased person. He would have had to undergo a period of ritual purification. But these details of purity and righteousness didn't bother Jesus. To him, the heart of the Gospel was compassion. He made room at the table for all, especially the ones society had marginalized.

William Sloane Coffin challenges those of us who try to follow Jesus to take seriously both the spiritual and the social dimensions of the gospel.

> Jesus was concerned most with those society counted least and put last. A politically engaged spirituality can never neglect the plight of those most deprived and vulnerable and will insist that improving the lot of the most oppressed is the decisive test of political sincerity. I believe in interreligious reverence, and believe further that a spiritual and ethical renewal of all the great religions of the world would be the greatest countervailing

> force to present-day economic interests that, in their pursuit of profits and growth, are so relentless as to make even governments more accountable to the market than to their own citizens.[31]

When I watch the TV preachers today what I hear in their message is a theology not of discipleship or sacrifice, but a theology of prosperity. They treat prayer like the children's letters to Santa Claus that appear in the local newspapers the week before Christmas. "I've been good. Bring me a pony." "If you accept Jesus as your personal Lord and Savior, the riches of our society can be yours. Your financial status will improve. You get your heavenly reward. Life will go better for you and you will escape the suffering that bogs down those who aren't as righteous as you are." The point of religion, they maintain, is a better life for you and your family. Religion is sold to us like a personal lifeboat to rescue us from the difficulties of this life. Save yourself.

The *Living the Questions* curriculum points out:

> What passes for Christianity today is really *two* different religions. One which encourages people to ask, "What can God do for me?" (save me, give me victory, make me prosperous and successful) and the other, "What can I do for God?" (what gifts have I been given to serve the less fortunate and change the world for the better?"). When someone asks you, "Are you saved?" what they mean is, "Have you had a personal experience of God's grace in your life so that you can accept Jesus as your personal Savior?" What they don't ask is "Have you been involved helping the poor in this world? Have you been feeding the hungry? Are you seeking justice for the oppressed?"[32]

It's obviously an attractive message for many people, this personal salvation faith—otherwise these guys wouldn't be on TV—but it's not a biblical message. Jesus came along offering an alternative vision. In contrast to political systems that thrive on domination, competition, and personal reward, Jesus put forward a politics of compassion, where the weaker, poorer, and more vulnerable members of society were to be lifted up and given a special place at the table. In fact, in one articulation of that vision, the poor were to be given good things to eat and the rich sent away hungry (Luke 1:53)—a complete reversal of the way we normally do politics. Of course, Jesus got in trouble for that. That was revolutionary talk against Caesar and the Roman Empire, and it got him killed. It's still an unpopular notion. Political candidates rarely get elected on a platform of sacrificing personal objectives for the common good. Usually the question asked of them is "What's in it for me?" They're forced to pander to the coalitions with the most money or the biggest voting block.

Jim Wallis, in his powerful book *God's Politics*, writes, "We have been buffeted by private spiritualities that have no connection to public life and a secular politics showing disdain for religion or even spiritual concerns. That leaves spirituality without social consequences and a politics with no soul."[33] He calls for a political renewal movement with the following basic beliefs:

- We believe that poverty—caring for the poor—is a religious issue.
- We believe that the environment—caring for God's earth—is a religious issue.
- We believe that war—and our call to be peacemakers—is a religious issue.
- We believe that truth-telling is a religious issue.
- We believe that human rights—respecting the image of God in every person—is a religious issue.
- We believe that our response to terrorism is a religious issue.
- We believe that a consistent ethic of human life is a religious issue.[34]

Wallis goes on to ask these rhetorical questions as a stinging critique to the way religion has been misused in partisan politics:

"When did Jesus become pro-war? When did Jesus become pro-rich? When did Jesus become a selective moralist?"

Former president Jimmy Carter agrees.

> There is an overwhelming religious mandate, often ignored by fundamentalists, to alleviate the plight of those who are in need. Jim Wallis, editor of *Sojourners* magazine, reports that he and a group of other seminary students searched the Bible to find every verse that referred to wealth and poverty. They were impressed to discover that one out of sixteen verses in the New Testament, one in ten in three of the gospels, and one in seven in the Gospel of Luke referred to money or to the poor. In the Hebrew Scriptures, only idolatry was mentioned more times than the relationship between rich and poor.
>
> When we recite the Lord's Prayer and pray for God's kingdom to come on earth, we are asking for an end to political and economic injustice within worldly regimes. . . . It is clear that proper treatment of the poor should be an extremely high priority among those who shape American policies.[35]

Jesus called people into community, reminding us that we need one another in order to survive and thrive. That's why we do church. Churches are volunteer communities where people are supported and challenged to be responsive to the needs around them, where they are helped to find hope in hopeless situations. At our best, in spite of pressure from the culture around us to the contrary, we don't sell personal fulfillment. We challenge people to social responsibility. Don't get me wrong. We are in favor of people finding personal fulfillment. It's just that we believe authentic personal fulfillment can only be discovered through service and sacrifice. It may not be fulfillment in terms of that new boat or fancy sports car or vacation house at the lake. But it will be fulfilling in terms of knowing you are invested in the most important human project there is—building community, touching lives. It's not about you. Albert Schweitzer wrote, "I don't know what your destiny will be, but one thing I do know: the only ones among you who will be really happy are those who have sought and found out how to serve."

Coffin writes,

> A church is a place where we try to think, speak, and act in God's way, not in the way of a fear-filled world. A church is a home for love, a home for brothers and sisters to dwell in unity, to rest and be healed, to let go their defenses and be free—free from worries, free from tensions, free to laugh, free to cry.[36]

It may seem odd to ask society to be more like an organized bicycle ride across the state of Iowa, but there you have it. The community that develops as cyclists from across the nation and around the world make their way from one side of the state to the other is a model for the church, which, in turn, is a glimpse of the realm of God and a paradigm for the way in which we should construct all human relations.

We are all connected and interdependent. A biblical faith reveals that we were created for community. There is no sense of the individual in biblical culture. People are first and foremost in relationship with others in a mutually supportive community. Like on RAGBRAI. RAGBRAI is a big extended family. There's a sense that we're all in this together. I may be getting wet cycling in this downpour, but so are ten thousand others around me on the road today. Burdens shared are lightened, and can be laughed about.

An experience like RAGBRAI exposes our vulnerabilities and gives people opportunities to take care of one another. It forces community on us, unaccustomed as we are to living in true interdependence, and makes community seem natural. It makes us better people, at least for a week each summer. Now and then we each need a push up a hill. Now and then we shouldn't be above pushing others.

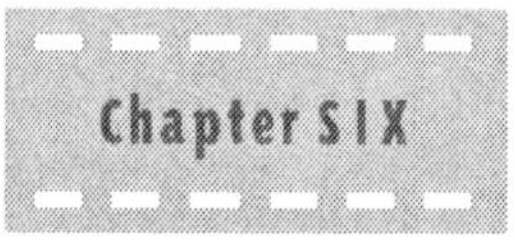

Snacks Are at the Top of the Hill

FOOD IS the great perk of RAGBRAI. You can encounter breakfast burritos, bananas, watermelon, corn on the cob, pork burgers, spaghetti dinners, snow cones, cold pickles, hot dogs, homemade cookies and cinnamon rolls, frozen Dove bars, pancakes, pies in all the colors of the rainbow, enough beer and Gatorade to float a battleship, lemonade, smoothies, pork chops, and, remarkably, organic fair trade coffees. And that's before you reach the first town in the morning. After a few days on the road your metabolism is cranked up to such a level that you can eat it all and still be hungry in an hour. You don't even gain any weight—at least not during the ride. But beware. Once the ride is over and you're no longer burning off three thousand calories a day, there will be a delay of a couple of days before your stomach gets the message. You'll still be eating like a finely tuned machine and you'll tend to blow up like a balloon. Carl Voss, an Iowan known for his love of pie, is quoted by John Karras as saying, "If you lose weight on RAGBRAI you are not having a good time."[37]

All these varied food items are for sale along the road, sold on street corners and farmsteads, and sometimes just out there in the sun at a crossroad in the country. Throughout the whole five hundred miles from river to river, you're never more than a few feet from another potential meal. Little kids sit behind lemonade stands for hours with hopeful expressions, and sometimes they make a killing. I can imagine a kid getting through college on the proceeds from one well-placed lemonade stand. Then there are the beefcake guys in shorts with no shirts, well-tanned with bushy blonde hair, mixing up lemonade by the side of the road. Don't think they don't clean up. Not to be outdone, the cappuccino girls are just down the road selling $5 shots of espresso and wearing little more than smiles and skimpy bikinis. There are high-class Dove bar stands and a stand with an old gasoline engine cranking homemade ice cream. There are pasta stands and homemade root beer stands. There is a food stand every several hundred yards along the road for four or five hundred miles. It's an incredible array.

But there's one common denominator among all the food booths—at least the successful ones—a curious fact: they're always at the top of the hill. You have to do your work before you get to eat or drink. If you do encounter a lemonade stand or a homemade pie booth at the bottom of a hill, you'll notice that few if any riders will stop there. It's too much trouble to get going again uphill. The unfortunate kids who live at the bottoms of hills and set up their lemonade stands there will retire in disgust a few hours into the day. Their well-laid plans to make enough to buy that new bike will come to nothing because they've neglected those three cardinal rules of sales: location, location, and location.

Snacks are at the top of the hill. Two lessons can be derived from this fact. The first has to do with delayed gratification, patience, and perseverance. The second lesson has to do with incentive. Sort of a carrot-and-stick set of lessons.

In terms of the first, you have to do your work before you get your snack. The writer of the New Testament Letter to the Hebrews says, "Let us lay aside every weight and the sin that clings so closely, and let us run with perseverance the race that is set before us, looking to Jesus the pioneer and perfecter of our faith (12:1-2)." The work of faithful discipleship is like a race run by an athlete. We're not just supposed to believe the right things about Jesus, we have to pick up our feet and run alongside him in this marathon of faith. Jesus said, "Take up your cross daily and follow me." Discipleship may be a difficult journey—just look at where it led Jesus—but the goal is intimacy with the divine. That's our silver lining, the light at the end of the tunnel. You have to get to the top of the hill before you can stop to suck on a snow cone. They're not going to give it to you in the valleys. There's always work to do, and it falls squarely on your shoulders.

My mother's way of saying the same thing was, "You have to clean your plate before you get your dessert."

One of my riding friends, Bob, thought he had discovered a shortcut one year on RAGBRAI. He and his wife, Meg, were both riding, but they had brought their car along as a support vehicle, and for some reason they had lost their driver. I don't mean misplaced him—although that tends to happen a lot on RAGBRAI, too—but he had to go home, or they couldn't make arrangements, or something like that. Anyway, one of them had to drive the vehicle while the other traveled by bike. They would switch off this responsibility like a tag-team wrestling match.

At first, driving the vehicle seemed like an odious chore. They had gotten this vacation time to ride RAGBRAI, not shepherd a vehicle across the state. Few people go along on RAGBRAI to drive. (My younger brother, however has been considering doing just that. We are trying to get him to come and drive a van and scope out the beer gardens and entertainment venues ahead of us. Maybe he'll even do our laundry for us. We think he'd enjoy it.) But when Bob was stuck with the car, he would meet Meg and me in the pass-through towns along the route where there were beer gardens and bands playing. We would find him, over and over again during the day, sitting under a tree with a contented look on his face and a beer in his hand, grooving on the music. I've never seen him so relaxed. He reckoned as how he might do RAGBRAI by car from then on. It sure was a lot less work. We talked him out of it precisely because of the lesson this chapter presents. It's just not the same if you get the rewards without doing the work. There is a genuine sweetness to life that is lessened when the discipline of working for it is removed.

One indication of the decline of modern society has to be our growing demand for instant gratification. Credit card debt is soaring, as are bankruptcies and foreclosures, while savings are at an all-time low. We want what we want when we want it, by God, and we're not going to be put off. My generation was worse in this regard than my parents' generation, but my kids' generation takes the cake. I used to ask my eighth grade confirmation students what they wanted to be when they grew up. I don't ask that question anymore because I have gotten too cynical over the years. The answers were always the same. "I want to make a hundred thousand dollars and buy a big boat (or truck)." That was back in the 1980s. Inflation probably has those dreams up to a quarter of a million dollars by now.

But, I'd press them, what do you feel called to *do*? What are you passionate about? What do you love enough to want to sacrifice for, to study for, to get into debt with school loans for? What has God created you for? How do you plan to be *useful* and *productive*?

"I don't know. I just want the money."

The United Church of Christ statement of faith calls disciples to accept both the joy and the cost of discipleship. That's a rare expectation in this day and age. That may be part of the reason that mainline denomination church membership is declining. We expect something out of members. Jesus said, "Take up your cross and follow me." We know the end of the story. We know where his faithful service led him. Prophets who speak the truth to power never get off easy. When churches preach a countercultural message, people who buy into that culture will either turn a deaf ear or come down hard on the agitator.

But the growing churches on the edge of town seem to offer an easier path to discipleship. If only you believe in God, they seem to say, and place your trust in Jesus as your personal Lord and Savior, your dreams will come true. Material wealth will be yours if you say the right magic words. Believe and prosper.

My progressive Baptist minister friend and I for a time were fascinated with the success of Rev. Joel Osteen, author of the bestselling book *Your Best Life Now*. His preaching is televised from Lakewood Church in Houston, Texas, which is in the renovated Compaq Center, a stadium seating sixteen thousand. Osteen fills it every week and reaches out to millions more through the television broadcast. We wanted to learn what it was that people were tuning in to. So we began watching and studying.

We heard Osteen say the most outlandish things and get away with it. He implied that if you had faith like he did, you could get a wife as pretty as his. (I got a wife at least as pretty as his, and my faith is nothing like his.) He preaches a theology of prosperity, which says that the faithful will succeed in everything they put their minds to, including the accumulation of wealth. Never mind that Jesus said "Go, sell what you own, and give the money to the poor, and you will have treasure in heaven" (Mark 10:21). Osteen said flat out that if you trust God, you'll get that prime parking space in front of the grocery story. I'm not kidding. Actually I do get those parking places now all the time, but it's not because of my faith. It's because of my handicap parking placard. Membership has its privileges.

That gospel of prosperity doesn't seem to be in my Bible. I've looked. In my Bible, the prophetic witness consistently calls for self-sacrifice for the common good. My Bible calls kings and rulers to account for neglecting the cause of the poor and marginalized. Nowhere does my Bible promise prosperity to the faithful. Rather, the faithful are those who serve. Jesus, the most obedient of them all, was crucified for his faithfulness. There were no perks for Jesus, no great parking places, no beautiful wife, no accumulation of wealth. And we're called to follow him.

There are no shortcuts. The snacks are at the top of the hill. You've got to crank your way to the top if you want to enjoy them.

Grinnell College in Iowa is the second most heavily endowed private college in America—only the venerable Harvard has a greater endowment. Grinnell has over a billion dollars in endowment, amassed due to generous giving by a graduate, Robert Noyce, who happened to be the coinventor of the computer microchip, and wise financial management by Warren Buffet. Grinnell College could afford to give a free education to every student enrolled. But the trustees, who have actually wrestled with this very issue, have wisely decided that an education that doesn't cost anything isn't worth anything. A student should want to come to Grinnell badly enough to be willing to pay for what the education is worth. The rewards are sweeter when you earn them by the sweat of your brow.

The fact that the snacks are always located at the top of the hill is not only an illustration of the perseverance called for in this life, but also hints at the incentives provided. Pavlov trained dogs that way. For a proper treat he could get animals to do almost anything, including autonomic responses like salivating. What does it take to get a RAGBRAI rider to salivate? Back in the early days of this great bike ride, a state highway patrol trooper who came along on the ride in order to provide security was fond of following groups of cyclists up a hill and shouting at them from his bullhorn, "There's watermelon at the top of the hill!" knowing full well there was nothing up there at all but more road. I can't speak to the state of mind of the riders when they crested the hill and discovered that he had lied to them (although I can certainly imagine), but I'm sure that his announcement would have given them a temporary boost up the hill. Was it coincidence that those early RAGBRAI years of the mid-1970s coincided with great tension between young radicals and law enforcement officers in cities across our nation? Perhaps word may have spread about this Iowa trooper's cruel hoax. All that unrest was simply a backlash.

In spite of everything I just said about having to work first in order to earn our rewards, I also affirm that life is sweet and that the sweetness is just around the bend (or, if you will, at the top of the hill). The life of faith is always drawn forward toward a reward of unimaginable richness. There's a better world out there. The promise of God is a life of harmony, compassion, and hospitality for all. Biblical people were always marching toward a better life.

In the time of Moses, a better life was envisioned by the Hebrew slaves in Egypt as a broad land flowing with milk and honey. That was an attractive image, because the Hebrew people had neither land of their own nor enough to eat. They had been enslaved in Egypt and conditions were becoming more and more harsh. In fact, Moses was called from his private life to lead them to freedom because God had heard their cries of suffering. Now they were en route to a homeland of their own.

Seven hundred years later, during the sixth century B.C. in the time of Isaiah, the dream was cast in terms of a place where lions would lie down with lambs and eat straw together, a place where human relations were defined by peaceful structures, where there would be no more crying. Think how attractive such an image would have been to a population exiled from their homeland and stranded far away in Babylon. The ruling class from ancient Israel had been deported when they were overrun by the Babylonians. They spent half a century longing for return. Their hopes were spelled out in language that harkened back to the Exodus. This would be a new and improved Exodus, with all creation restored. And finally, in the time of Jesus, the dream was articulated in terms of reconciliation and intimacy with God. Not only would there be liberation from Roman domination, but there would be a cosmic reordering of creation. There would be nothing to separate us from the love of God, neither in life nor in death.

Just what is the final reward that Christians are looking forward to? What is the point of the Christian life? The answer to this question, perhaps more than any other, tends to divide Christians into two camps. For some, the answer is crystal clear. The goal toward which we have been struggling, that which will make the sacrifices of this life worth having put up with, is that we will go to heaven after we die. "We're going to a better place." And then, if pressed, most who answer this way will go on to describe just what heaven will look like. We will meet people we have loved in this life. Our knees won't ache any more. We'll be happy. I'll score that hole-in-one. This vision used to be pictured as a city whose streets are paved with gold. Nowadays we talk in terms of reconciling relationships. See Mitch Albom's *The Five People You Meet In Heaven* for a best-selling illustration.

Others answer the question about the point of Christian life by noting that, as with so many of the concepts we casually take for granted in our conventional grasp of religion, this idea of heaven is not a particularly biblical view. The Bible nowhere describes heaven as family reunion, a place we go after we die to meet up with family members who have gone before us. The Bible is much more interested in how we live in this life. Do we live with integrity? Do we treat people as we would want to be treated? Do we work for just social and political systems where even the most vulnerable citizens are recognized as having worth? That's what the Bible cares about. Really, our Judeo-Christian faith is very earthy. Every Sunday in my church we pray, "Thy kingdom come on earth, as it is in heaven." Never mind that everybody says it wrong, placing the comma after the word "come" rather than the word "earth." What the prayer of Jesus calls for is for God to establish the realm of peace and reconciliation right here and now, where we live. John Dominic Crossan says "Heaven is already in good shape; what we pray for is that the kingdom of God may also be on earth"[38]

There are few concrete claims made in the Bible about the afterlife. Clearly, there can be no certainty. What we do know is that we live and die in the presence of God. "If we live, we live to the Lord; and if we die, we die to the Lord. So then, whether we live or whether we die, we are the Lord's" (Romans 14:8). Marcus Borg writes,

> We can know what salvation means in this life. At the center of the biblical understanding of salvation is a relationship with God in the present, whose gifts are freedom, joy, peace, and love, and whose fruits are compassion and justice.

> This relationship with God, and all that flows from it, are the purpose of the Christian life. The invitation of the Christian gospel is to enter into that relationship in which our healing and wholeness lie, that relationship which transforms us by beginning to heal the wound of existence and makes our lives in the here and now a life with God.[39]

A pivotal claim of Jesus was "I come that they may have life, and have it abundantly" (John 10:10). That abundant life is amply described throughout the scriptures. It's a place of harmonious relationships, radical welcome and fair treatment for all, joy and peace. It's community, cooperation, and fun. I assume it would include bikes and beer, although they aren't specifically mentioned by name in the Bible. For me, if that's what is at the top of the hill, I'll eagerly crank my way up there. And if it's just cold watermelon, well, that will do for starters. A chunk of ice cold watermelon for a hot, tired cyclist is like a slice of heaven.

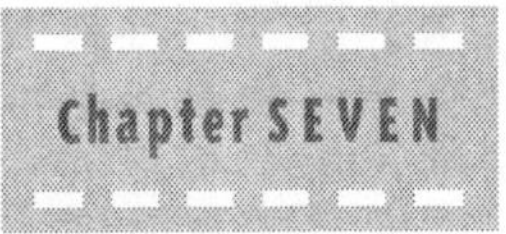

Chapter SEVEN

At Least Five Hundred Miles of Training: The Lost Art of Discipline

YOU SHOULD get in at least five hundred miles of training before the start of RAGBRAI every summer. That's what the organizers will tell you. There's a column posted on the RAGBRAI website written by a fitness expert who gives up-to-the-minute, down-to-the-wire advice on training for the ride, in the minutest detail. You need to get your leg muscles strong enough to pump the miles and the hills. You need to get your body used to undergoing several hours of activity. You have to learn how to fuel the machine for that long. And there's no way around the demands on your rear end. Everything has to be toughened up.

In my pre-accident days I used to put in two or three times the recommended amount. I was in such good shape that RAGBRAI was just a blip on the training radar screen. Even now on the handcycle I usually get in at least the recommended mileage. But I know for a fact you can do it on a lot less. One year my daughter did it on a total of thirty-five miles training. I just couldn't get her out to train. My wife is the same way. Ann and I set out once (this was way back, B.C. as we like to say—"Before Children") on a one thousand mile bike tour from Iowa to Alabama. She had exactly seventeen miles of training under her belt. Wonder where my daughter gets it.

My daughter didn't have a thought in her pretty little head about the need to prepare for something before doing it. "Train for RAGBRAI? Are you kidding? It's hot out there! And I don't want to mess up my hair." But she managed to cover all the miles on RAGBRAI, including the optional one-hundred-mile day, because she's young and the young can do crazy, irresponsible things and get away with it. She was, however, awfully crabby the whole week on the ride. Which was all my fault, she concluded.

Whenever I try to skimp on my training, I notice one thing: the ride isn't any fun. You do the training so that you can enjoy the experience with a minimum of discomfort. RAGBRAI is not much fun if you're so sore you can't move by the end of the day and if you're so beat down by the heat and the hills that you can't dance or enjoy the beer and the pie. You train so you can play. You work hard so you can enjoy the fruits of your labors. Remember the previous chapter? The snacks are at the top of the hill. You have to get up there, somehow, before you can imbibe.

One important training goal I put in place every year in preparation for RAGBRAI is to gradually increase my intake of carbonated alcoholic beverages. Normally, I drink very little beer. If I'm not careful, I'll purchase a six pack of beer in August and find four bottles left over next June. That's when I panic because I realize that I haven't trained nearly hard enough for RAGBRAI. So, at some point in the spring I'll start drinking beer. I'll start slow, one bottle a week maybe for the first couple of weeks. Then a couple of bottles a week. By the start of July I should be able to comfortably polish off a beer a day, or I'll be in trouble when it's time to start the ride the last week in July. Fortunately, beer is a lot easier to drink under the hot sun after seventy miles of bike riding than it is on a dark winter day.

My riding partner, Bob, and I worried about our training for the 2000 ride. We were both with our church youth group on a mission experience in Mexico for the two weeks before

RAGBRAI was to start. We wouldn't be able to get any miles in at all. But Bob came up with a solution. He figured that the intense heat of working under the hot Mexican sun on our building project would certainly help him acclimatize to the Iowa heat and humidity. And he also reasoned that he could toughen up his butt for the hard, narrow bicycle seat simply by sitting on a narrow concrete block for several hours every day. His training regime worked. He said he'd never had an easier time on the ride.

But the best training story I've heard, quoted in John Karras's book, was from a rider named Lorraine Roth. She wrote,

> Rather than working on physical exertion I concentrate for two weeks on developing survival skills, including nutritional and schedule variations. Ingesting a daily pint of Crisco, alternating liquid and solid forms, prepares my digestive system for the endless porkburgers and hamburgers that are to come. An additional half-dozen cookies and two or three quarts each of iced tea, lemonade, and water are also minimum daily requirements.
>
> In anticipation of the week's rituals, my daily routines also are altered. My alarm rings at 3:30 a.m. I push "play" on my tape deck, and "Campgrounds Sounds I" begins. The familiar sounds of clanking tent stakes, alarm clocks at five-minute intervals, and cries of "Come on, Jody, we're burning daylight!" fill the air. A teenager screams as a tent is let down on top of her, followed by loud laughter.
>
> Arising at 5 a.m., I get dressed, make my bed, then stand outside my bathroom door for 37 minutes before entering. I repeat this procedure several times a day. Then, at 4:35 p.m., after my 37-minute wait, I take a breathtakingly icy shower, taking care that the water is cold enough to require a full 10 minutes to rinse out shampoo, with teeth clenched, breath held.
>
> In the evenings, I sit or lie on the floor, and stand by the telephone for 45 minutes before making a call. At the

end of the day, I climb into my sleeping bag on the hardwood floor, first having made sure the marbles are strategically placed. I play Side 2 of "Campground Sounds"—similar to Side 1, but with the addition of foul language as bikers trip over tent ropes.

At the end of this strict diet and rigorous training, I am truly prepared for the ride.[40]

If RAGBRAI takes some preparation, then so should life. I don't think society should let people attempt life without a proper training course. You need to pass a test to get a driver's license, after all. I require several hours of premarital counseling before I'll conduct a wedding for a couple. Shouldn't we need some sort of certification for the project of life? M. Scott Peck begins his book *The Road Less Traveled* with this revelation: "Life is difficult. This is a great truth, one of the greatest truths. It is a great truth because once we truly see this truth, we transcend it."[41]

He believes that most people refuse to recognize this basic fact about life, wishing and make believing that life is easy, or at least that it should be. With an attitude like that, every challenge becomes a direct affront, a tragedy, an affliction. That leads people to complain rather than undertake to resolve the difficulties.

"Life is a series of problems," Peck continues. "Do we want to moan about them or solve them? . . . Discipline is the basic set of tools we require to solve life's problems. Without discipline we can solve nothing. . . . With total discipline we can solve all problems." Of course, with that last statement he makes a religion out of his assertions, but you get the point. He goes on to argue that human development and maturity only take place when obstacles are met with discipline. All of life is a learning curve and an opportunity for growth if we choose to tackle it head on. "It is through the pain of confronting and resolving problems that we learn. As Benjamin Franklin said, 'Those things that hurt, instruct.'"[42]

Discipline is the exercise of doing something you don't particularly want to be doing at the moment—there are more attractive options out there—for the sake of a greater reward in the future. It's delayed gratification. I didn't particularly want to drag myself out of bed this morning at five in order to plug away at this book before going to my office for the day. I would much rather, at the moment, have stayed in bed listening to our classical music station on the radio and dreaming of fame and fortune. But, over the years, I've learned that fame and fortune won't come to me unless I get up and do the requisite work first. Even then it's iffy. If I've decided that it's a good thing to produce this book, which I have, then I have to rein in my natural tendencies toward sloth, and sit down and write. Discipline is the commitment to sacrifice momentary pleasures for the sake of a larger reward out there in the distance somewhere. At the top of the hill, let's say.

Discipline is getting up for church on Sunday morning because of the value of going to church, even if you were out late Saturday night and you don't feel like getting up. Discipline is declining that extra piece of dessert, even though it sure looks good, because you don't want to gain weight. Discipline is telling your child no, she can't stay out late, even though you know you're going to have a huge fight on your hands. Good parents say no lots, even though the first few times may provoke massive confrontations. Bad parents avoid the momentary confrontations and thus risk raising a child who is self-indulgent and superficial. Discipline is putting in the extra time at work to finish an important project, because you know that your sacrifice of time will lead to advancement. We exercise discipline in countless ways every day. Some of us are better at it than others.

A newborn baby is a bundle of need, absolute dependence. A baby needs to eat, and she needs to eat now. Her needs have to be met, right now, or you'll hear about it. And that's okay for babies. We wouldn't want them any other way. As children grow and mature, they learn to defer gratification as they exercise discipline. Well, some of them do. You've surely seen kids at the grocery store with their parents, kids who don't seem to have learned that lesson. They whine for what they want until their enabling parents give in and get it for them. And then, when they turn eighteen or twenty-one, they're loosed on the world and another generation of superficial, demanding, self-centered infants enters society.

One of the transferable values of athletic pursuit is familiarity with discipline. Athletes are used to training through discomfort and pain. No one would willingly endure what dedicated athletes endure on a regular basis if it weren't for the dream of better performance. The time for regular training must be taken out of the day. Pushing the threshold of endurance over and over again is painful, but it produces a more fit athlete, better able to endure the pain of competition.

At the same time that I'm pressed to produce the manuscript for this book, I'm training for the 2006 Chicago marathon. Both manuscript and marathon come due within a week of each other. Each endeavor demands solid discipline, with each competing for the same precious hours during the day (my parishioners apparently have certain expectations of me, too). My marathon training this month, the last month before the race, calls for long pushes in my racing chair, with ever-increasing intensity of effort. What I'm training for is the ability to continue to push fast even an hour-and-a-half into the event, when my muscles are fatigued and my body is screaming, "Stop, let me off!" There's absolutely no way to train for that effect, which I will desperately need in the final miles of the marathon, without first getting tired. It takes a two-hour workout at an increasing output of effort throughout.

I plan this workout all week. I know that on my day off, I'll have to get up early, pack my gear, and drive up to the bike trail. Then I'll get out of the car, transfer into my racing chair, and start pumping. I know it will be a painful experience. By the end of the second hour I'll be in a world of hurt. I know it will affect the whole rest of the day, that, in effect, I'll be paying for this effort all day—if not all weekend. Sometimes I'm almost not up to the sacrifice. But I have made a decision that I'm going to compete in the race, striving for a time that will at least qualify me for the Boston Marathon. Having made that decision, the discipline of training, however odious, is simply a given.

I'm convinced that my athletic discipline is one of the factors that made it possible for me to return to an active life following my "disabling" accident. When I returned to consciousness in the hospital after six weeks in a coma, I was barely able to lift my arms off the bed. I couldn't sit up or move myself. It took a great deal of determination and perseverance to push myself through physical therapy and rebuild muscles that had atrophied. When I was released from the hospital into a world that wasn't exactly designed for wheelchairs, I not only had to continue learning and strengthening, but I had to do it in the discouraging context of a malevolent—or at best indifferent—world. There were no awards given for successful accommodation. There were barriers, both physical and psychological, at every turn. For some time I had to keep reminding myself, "Put your head down, plow ahead, do what you have to." That had been my training mantra during workouts; now it became my mantra for rehabilitation. It was a marathon of adjustment measured in years rather than miles.

Several years ago I was called by the local hospital to visit another patient of theirs, a man who had been in an accident and, like me, was now in a wheelchair. They were concerned about his attitude; it seemed he was having difficulty moving on with his life. So I paid him a pastoral visit at his home.

I found him lying in a hospital bed set up in his living room. It was the middle of the afternoon and he was watching soap operas on TV and drinking beer out of the can with a straw. Now, I'm a professional. I can still be pastoral regardless of my personal feelings toward a situation. I have to confess that I was very judgmental as I rolled into this scene. What was this man's problem? Why didn't he get up and do something productive?

We sat and talked for awhile. I enjoyed getting to know him. He offered me a beer, which I accepted out of politeness, and we watched the soap opera. I had always drawn the line on afternoon TV. Even at my weakest, in the hospital, I made sure the TV was turned off when the soap operas came on. Even in my darkest hour, I had some sense of discipline. But, once you get into the plot, these things can be kind of engaging. He explained whose baby Jessica was carrying and who Brad was messing around with on the side and why Collin had never come home since that fateful night two years ago. We had another round of beers. And before I knew it, the afternoon was gone. And it had been rather pleasant.

Which caused me to wonder: Why did I have to push so hard to overcome, succeed, and produce, when there were perfectly viable lifestyles out there based on nothing but instant gratification? But then the beer buzz wore off and my old sense of discipline kicked in and I was myself again. I reminded myself that a life with at least a modicum of self-control is going to be a happier life at some level.

Richard J. Foster writes, "Superficiality is the curse of our age. The doctrine of instant satisfaction is a primary spiritual problem. The desperate need today is not for a greater number of intelligent people, or gifted people, but for deep people."[43]

He's right. We are a society of folks for whom immediate gratification has become a way of life, a religion almost. I met a young woman once who could have been a poster child for superficial. She had that California glow about her, tanned, fit, energetic, physical, attractive. She was an aerobics instructor (well of course she was). She never went to church, but she had been really into crystals lately. She did tarot card readings. But she was very interested in my background in overseas community development and parish ministry. At the end of our conversation she had made up her mind to become a missionary. What did she need to do to get started, she wanted to know.

How should I put this? Find a historic faith community and learn from them what has helped them and thousands of previous generations just like them face life. Scratch beneath the surface of your superficial cultural expressions and dig for meaning. You have to have a life-changing commitment to something before you can realistically expect to share it with others. Besides, you wouldn't like being a missionary. There's no hot water and you wouldn't be able to do a *thing* with your hair.

Signs of superficiality are all around us. Personal savings are at an all-time low because people can't seem to put off buying what they feel they need right now in order to save for the future. Back when I got married, couples were usually renting apartments and driving old used cars, barely making ends meet. Now, most of the young people I marry have already bought their houses and they're driving fancier cars than I've ever owned. Of course, their debt burdens are greater than I've ever carried, too. I just read a newspaper report about a new trend in grocery shopping. It's called serial shopping. We used to go to the grocery store once a week and load up a whole shopping cart full of food and supplies for the next several days. Now, busy shoppers pick up what they feel like having for supper tonight. They'll come back tomorrow for tomorrow's needs.

The "gaming industry" (the word "gambling" is still suspect in our society, so the industry uses the more friendly word, "gaming," to identify itself) is one of the fastest growing industries in our country today. I recall a time when gambling was considered sinful, and barely tolerated. Now there are casinos everywhere. There seems to be a growing craving among people to get rich quick. The ads for casinos show happy, smiling people having a good time rolling dice or pulling handles on slot machines, but when I've visited casinos all I see are driven, lonely individuals, hunched over their "game" in a smoky, noisy room, hell-bent on winning that jackpot so they won't have to go home and tell their wives and kids that they just lost the rent money. Again. Gambling, the urge to get rich quick, has become central to our culture. They announce the results of daily and weekly lottery drawings on the nightly news, and an extra-large jackpot can produce national headlines. State budgets have become addicted to the revenue that gambling produces.

Down on the Gulf Coast of Mississippi, residents are still trying to rebuild following the devastation of hurricanes Katrina and Rita. It's a slow, painful process. There is still mile after mile of private homes in ruins because funding hasn't materialized to help residents, many of whom were desperately poor, rebuild. But there was no delay in rebuilding the casinos that line the coast. They have rebounded with vigor, because there's money driving their recovery.

Popular fairy tales like Cinderella and Sleeping Beauty aren't just children's stories. They are unfortunately real-life strategies for many people. In the movie *Pretty Woman*, Julia Roberts plays a character who is picked up off the street and rescued in the end by Richard Gere, her knight in shining armor. We wait for salvation from a handsome prince or a fairy godmother. Many people play scripts from such fairy tales in their minds. They see the problems in their lives as too numerous to tackle. They feel powerless, on their own, to solve them. So they wait for their ship to come in, or for their one lucky break, or for the woman or man of their dreams to straighten them out. They put their lives on hold waiting for a lifeboat to be lowered and their lives turned around. What I'm describing is a wasted life, and I suspect it happens far too often.

Authentic, joyful living takes discipline. Christian spirituality throughout the ages has long been aware of this fact. You can't live a fulfilling life just responding to the whims of the moment. In order to be attentive to what's really important in life, you need some practice of discernment. That "still, small voice of God" that Elijah heard in his mountain hiding place can't reach us through the din of contemporary society. We surround ourselves with busyness, with noise, and with needs. Only when all this is swept away, even if only for brief, planned moments, can we begin to see that there may be something more to this life than we had been led to believe. The soil has to be prepared to receive it. The heart has to be trained.

Prayer is one of the ways that Christians have always disciplined themselves to be attentive to God's presence and will. Prayer isn't just asking God for things or to fix yourself or others. Prayer is fundamentally listening, not talking. Henri Nouwen says

> Prayer is the discipline of listening to that voice of love. Jesus spent many nights in prayer listening to the voice that had spoken to him at the Jordan River. We too must pray. Without prayer, we become deaf to the voice of love and become confused by the many competing voices asking for our attention. How difficult this is! When we sit down for half an hour—without talking to someone, listening to music, watching television, or reading a book—and try to become very still, we often find ourselves so overwhelmed by our noisy inner voices that we can hardly wait to get busy and distracted again. Our inner life often looks like a banana tree full of jumping monkeys! But when we decide not to run away and stay focused, these monkeys may gradually go away because of lack of attention, and the soft gentle voice calling us the beloved may gradually make itself heard.[44]

Repetition, chant, reciting a familiar prayer can have a centering, calming effect on the spirit. "Why is the attentive repetition of a well-known prayer so helpful in setting our hearts on the kingdom?" Nouwen asks. "It is helpful because the words of such a prayer have the power to transform our inner anxiety into inner peace."[45] I had a dark period in my ministry once, during which I found little joy. I was going through the motions, probably doing a decent job from the perspective of my parishioners, but nonetheless depressed about the whole vocation of ministry. I felt like a squirrel, scampering from one crisis to another, doing nothing meaningful except gathering nuts. During this time I stumbled across Psalm 46. "Be still, and know that I am God." God encourages the writer of the psalm to surrender control of his life to the Sovereign, to trust that God is in charge. The world is in the hands of God. We're not ultimately responsible for everything that happens. Be still. You're in good hands. I found myself repeating those lines often. And each time I did, I noticed a definite calming. I think this discipline saved me much anxiety during this difficult time.

Compassion is a discipline. There is much in our society that breaks down community and encourages us to center on ourselves at the expense of our neighbor. We are pitted against one another in competition for scarce resources. We treat life more like a Tour de France, where riders compete to be the first to arrive on the Champs Élysées in Paris, than like RAGBRAI, where riders move along as a team. We are made to feel as if those with whom we disagree are our enemies. We are surrounded by cultural myths extolling the virtues of materialism and individualism. It takes a conscious decision to unfetter yourself from these siren voices. Nouwen, again, says,

> To make compassion the bottom line of life, to be open and vulnerable to others, to make community life the focus, and to let prayer be the breath of your life . . . that requires a willingness to tear down the countless walls that we have erected between ourselves and others in order to maintain our safe isolation. This is a lifelong and arduous spiritual battle because while tearing down walls with one hand, we build new ones with the other. True conversion asks for a lot more than a change of place. It asks for a change of heart.[46]

The same sort of diligence in training that I willingly undergo in order to prepare for RAGBRAI each year is what Nouwen advocates for the life of faith. It takes a rock-solid commitment and daily exercise. What would life be like to read the daily papers with a heart of compassion for the victims of those countless crimes and calamities, and then, rather than wallowing in pity or insulating ourselves in order to escape the pain of it all, we devoted ourselves to community-building. In other words, what if we were to actually live what we profess to believe?

Other disciplines can be just as effective. Spiritual guides will encourage disciples to journal about their feelings, to read scripture or spiritual writings attentively, to worship within a supportive community. There are many techniques. The point of each of them is to help the practitioner become more attentive to the presence of God, more appreciative of the world around, and more aware of the fellow travelers at our side.

We're not very good at that these days. We tend to just skim the surface, like a water bug on a pond, never breaking any deeper. Don't think Madison Avenue isn't aware of this superficiality. Advertisers thrive on it. We chase after one fashion after another, in hot pursuit of the latest fads. Discipline is a lost art, an unpopular hindrance for a people hooked on instant gratification. If we can't pop it in the microwave, we don't have time for it. It is quite accepted these days to live moment to moment. It's the examined life that is uncommon.

But just as RAGBRAI won't be as much fun if you don't have at least a few hundred miles of training behind you, so life is impoverished without some sort of discipline. Sure you can do it—many people do—but in order to fully experience the gift of abundant life offered by God, we have to curb the ego and painstakingly prepare the soil of the soul.

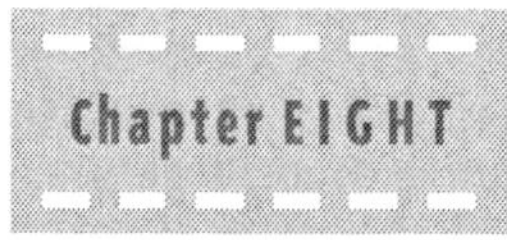

Push Your Frontiers

TWO YEARS after my accident I made an accidental commitment to ride every mile of RAGBRAI by handcycle. I had ridden about half of each day's ride the previous year, and even that had been a stretch. I was still only about nine months out of the hospital and my stamina left much to be desired. But I'd been training through the following winter and spring, and this year I was going to go for the whole thing. It wasn't really my idea, and I would have preferred not to have had to make the commitment, but I was forced into it.

A local TV news station had heard about me. They wanted to do an interview. The camera crew caught up with me while I was out on a training ride. "So," the perky young reporter wanted to know, "you're going to ride every mile this year?"

I was trapped. What could I say? The gauntlet had been thrown and I could not help but pick it up. "Of course, I'm going for the whole thing." Now all I had to do was produce. I trained and I trained, and when July came around I gritted my teeth and set out on the first leg of the trip.

The ride started innocently enough, on the flatlands of the great northwestern Iowa prairie. For three or four days of idyllic riding, the largest hill was the highway overpass over Interstate 35 going north into Minnesota. We rolled along pleasantly enough. Even though the heat was bothersome, the task seemed manageable. But the route wound up in northeast Iowa, the home of the dreaded Iowa Alps. This is the corner of the state where the hardy Scandinavian pioneers had settled because the steeply rolling hills reminded them of home. They breed cows up there with left legs shorter than right legs so the animals can stand level on the hillsides. No, really—I read it on the Internet.

On Friday we woke up in Decorah and got on the road at 5 a.m. There was no level stretch of highway anywhere. Some of the hills rolled on for two or three miles, winding out of sight around the trees and getting steeper with every bend. I cranked up some of them so slowly that cyclists who were dismounting in order to walk their bikes up the hill were passing me. The heat was also unbearable. By midafternoon a thermometer hanging off the back of one guy's bike registered over 100 degrees. The asphalt road surface turned to soupy, sticky tar.

I was out on the road for thirteen hours, cranking steadily.

But I had made my commitment and I was, by golly, going to stick with it.

My wife, Ann, who you might notice is never mentioned in my RAGBRAI stories, was not on the ride that year. She's never on the ride anymore. She used to ride with me, but the heat and the physical effort bothered her. So now she stays home. This particular year, she had gone east to visit her sister in Springfield, Massachusetts. She spent her vacation dining on Maine lobster and listening to the Boston Symphony and shopping for antiques. We have diametrically opposed ideas as to what constitutes fun.

Who had the better vacation, she wanted to know upon her return. Ann is a much better critic of my choices than she is a companion on my adventures.

Choose your challenges carefully, she advises me. Just because you can accomplish a great feat, what does the accomplishment say about your goals and values? Was it fun? Was it worth it? Does it pay your salary? Once I actually won $300 in a bike race. But when I brought my winnings home and declared I was going to retire from parish ministry to pursue professional sports, she scoffed. "Why do you feel the need to push all the time?" she asked. "Why can't you just relax? Read a book. Take up knitting. Play cards. Come with me to shop for antiques. You know, things that normal people do."

But dear, I point out sweetly, shouldn't we push every boundary and explore every avenue, climb every mountain and ford every stream, until we find our dream? After all, that's how life populated this planet, pushing into every crack and crevice imaginable. I recently saw a television documentary about a type of octopus that lives at such depths in the ocean that its environment is pitch black. It finds its food by sticking tentacles into holes in the ocean floor, hoping to find prey. Every once in awhile it pokes into the den of an eel or snapping crustacean, which promptly lops off its tentacle. No matter. It just grows another one. I saw that as a metaphor for exploring life. We need to test out any and every opportunity. No matter that some of them are challenging and dangerous. If our legs get bitten off, or damaged in a car accident, we'll just grow new ones—I mean find a wheelchair—and continue on our way. As our children grow up we encourage them to try out band and sports and drama and academics and dance, not knowing which will be their passion and vocation, but knowing that they will grow through the exercise and challenge of each.

Now I was on a roll. I wasn't so sure I'd scored any points with the story about the octopus, but I knew she couldn't argue against the welfare of children.

I come from a small Midwestern town that really supports its local high school. Every fall there is a homecoming weekend, which includes the home football game, the homecoming dance where the kids get all gussied up and spend lots of money looking sophisticated for an evening, and the traditional homecoming parade. In our little town, the parade has a unique characteristic. Every club, organization, and sport from the high school is represented, along with the requisite tractors and fire trucks and local car dealers and politicians. But the school is so small that most of the kids participate in several different activities. Some kids play in sports that overlap. Some even play football and then march in the band at halftime. Many participate in drama or choir on top of everything else. All these commitments create a problem when it comes time for the parade. Which float will they ride on? But the kids have found a solution. It's a long parade, what with all the tractors and politicians and insurance agencies, so when one unit finishes at central park, the kids who are in other organizations just hop off that first unit, throw on another jersey or uniform, and scurry off to find their second unit. Then they ride that one to the end. I've known kids from my church who have hopped onto three different floats over the course of one parade. You've got to admire these kids. Not only will their resumes help them get into more competitive colleges, but they will have experienced a variety of sports, disciplines, and activities by the time they have to commit to one course of study or preparation.

Sometimes it is important to explore every option that presents itself. When I was undergoing physical therapy following my accident, there was no way of knowing how far I might progress. There is no predicting how the body will recover, or if there will be further nerve regeneration, and there's no telling what level of mobility a newly injured patient might be capable of back in the world. So we experimented with a variety of assistive devices. My basement is a graveyard of discarded technology—cumbersome leg braces, canes and crutches and walkers. It looks like a miraculous healing shrine where the faithful have been cured and abandoned their crutches. Some of the experiments have played out and have been incorporated into my life. Others didn't mesh with my lifestyle, so I abandoned them and moved on. I found, for example, that I could walk with assistance using lightweight ankle braces, but it wasn't a practical solution for going long distances. It was also impractical to carry around the walker I needed with the braces. So the braces are just a handy solution to the problem of getting on airplanes, buses, and into inaccessible homes with stairs. I'm glad I explored all the options. From time to time, I reevaluate my level of activity and try to determine if other sorts of commitments might be more useful.

I remind my wife about all the important discoveries that have been made accidentally by inventors, scientists, and explorers who were looking for one thing and found something completely different. Thomas Edison, it is said, experimented with thousands of different materials to use for a filament in his new invention, the light bulb, before he stumbled across one that worked most efficiently. Although he wasn't the first to actually invent the incandescent bulb, he fiddled persistently enough with all the factors involved to produce a viable product. For the earliest filaments he tried everything from string to bamboo. Then he had to try various gases in the bulb. But what finally clinched the deal was being able to supply a consistent source of electricity and hook it all together in a network. Did his wife say, "Quit fiddling with those filaments and get a real job!"? No, she was supportive of her husband's tinkering. At least, that's how I tell it to Ann.

Christopher Columbus failed to find the western passage to China that he sought for trade. There was a huge land mass in the way and the distances were vastly greater than he had imagined. But he did open up the Americas to European exploration. Of course, there are those who still wish he had stayed home. Be that as it may, did his wife say, "Chris, now where are you going? I need your help around the house"? We don't really know, but if she did, Christopher set sail anyway.

Some of our most effective drugs were developed by accident while a scientist was trying to create something completely different. When researchers were searching for a culture in which to rapidly grow the new antibiotic, penicillin, they searched high and low until they found the ideal environment in a moldy cantaloupe in Peoria. Who'd have thought?

Georges Bizet, the French composer, wrote thirty operas before he produced a hit. He died, at the age of thirty-six, the year his most famous opera, *Carmen*, premiered. Did his wife say, "Why don't you write something practical, like greeting cards or advertising copy?" He kept at his dream. We all need to keep trying. We need to keep pushing. I think I need to keep riding RAGBRAI.

Ann says I'm just rationalizing. But I still think I'm onto something here.

A few years later she planned a trip to Ireland with her mother and sisters during the RAGBRAI week.

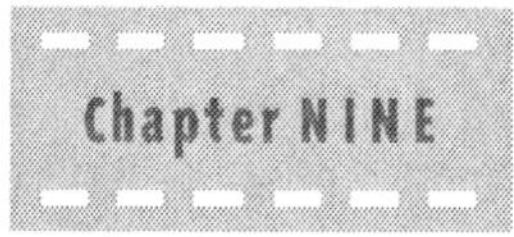

When All Is Said and Done

TWENTY-FIVE people have died on RAGBRAI over the years. The fear that one of the bicyclists might actually die on the ride used to keep the organizers up at night, lying there in a cold sweat. The fact there were no fatalities at all for the first eleven years of the ride now seems like a statistical anomaly. The organizers were lucky. Twenty-five deaths may seem like a lot, until you do the math and realize it's less than one fatality per year. Whenever you get fifteen thousand people together for a week doing anything, chances are there will be mortality.

Still, it seems so unexpected and unfair during an experience like RAGBRAI. After all, we ride RAGBRAI in order to beat the odds. We ride to lower our cholesterol, or to lose weight so we might live longer and healthier lives. And yet death strikes even on this most life-affirming of experiences. How does this affect our thinking? For many, it shakes the very foundations.

Most of the deaths have been related to heart attacks or to other preexisting health problems, or to accidents not directly related to cycling. That makes these deaths no less devastating for family and friends, but somewhat more understandable. Only three RAGBRAI deaths have been actually cycling-related. Remarkably, I happened to be among the first on the scene for two mishaps that resulted in fatalities, and the third involved the father of a close friend. More on that later.

Death pulls a somber curtain over the entire ride. "There but for the grace of God go I." A man was killed in a storm a couple of years ago when a tree branch fell on his tent, just a block or two away from where my two grown children were camping. We saw the limb the next morning, still lying on top of his crushed tent. And during the very next day of riding, due to lack of sleep from the storm, my kids collided on the road in an accident that sent my daughter to the hospital with a concussion. My brother and I rode a harrowing ten miles back against the flow of bicycle traffic to the small town hospital where she had been taken. She recovered, but her ride was over for the week. If she hadn't been wearing her helmet her brains would have been splattered on the highway. And of course, my own life was nearly ended in 1997 while I was training for the ride. People die on bikes, just as they die at war and in traffic accidents and in fires and in bed.

The father of a good friend of mine was killed the night before the ride started in 2000. It was to have been a glorious father-son ride. Their story is a fitting illustration of both the devastating tragedy and the unexpected grace of sudden death.

My friend, Doug Cutchins, is an administrator at Grinnell College. He runs the Office of Social Commitment, and under his leadership Grinnell College has become among the top institutions, per capita, in terms of numbers of alumni who have become Peace Corps volunteers. He and his wife, Anne, wrote a book called *Volunteer Vacations*, a guide to volunteer service placement organizations. He's energetic, concerned for peace and justice both professionally and personally, and, like me, a former Peace Corps volunteer. So we connected when he came to town.

Doug recounts that when he first came to Grinnell as a college freshman, his roommate had ridden RAGBRAI the summer before classes started. Doug and his dad, Carl, thought the ride sounded fun. They vowed to do it together some day.

Well, "some day" got postponed. Doug graduated from college before he got around to doing the ride. He did the Peace Corps thing. Then, as luck would have it, he found his way back to Grinnell as a college administrator. Finally he and his dad were able to set a date to ride together in 2000.

Carl Cutchins was the son and grandson of Methodist preachers. He attended Yale Divinity School and planned on a career in the ministry, but found he was more interested in counseling. He earned his MSW and eventually became Executive Director of the Northampton Center for Children in Northampton, Massachusetts, a nonprofit corporation providing residential treatment, special education, and outpatient services to emotionally disturbed children, adolescents, and their families. After his death, the center was renamed the Cutchins Programs for Children and Families, Inc.

At the moment the idea for the ride was hatched, Carl didn't even have a serviceable bike. He had in the basement a thirty-year-old Schwinn that hadn't seen the light of day for years. So he bought a bike and started riding to work and taking longer weekend trail rides. Carl wasn't a trained athlete, but he was no slouch. He had this habit of getting turned on by the sports his grown children were engaged in. "If we kids got involved in a sport, he'd jump on board," Doug says. Doug's sister took up SCUBA. So Carl got certified in SCUBA. Doug ran the 1993 Twin Cities Marathon in Minneapolis. Carl came up as support crew, got hooked, and then ran the 1995 Marine Corps Marathon in Washington, DC. RAGBRAI was a natural. It was going to be the ultimate father-son ramble.

The week before the ride, Carl wasn't feeling well. He went to his doctor complaining of chest pains, but nothing showed up on the tests. He flew out to Iowa Friday, July 21st, and spent the night with his son in Grinnell. It was already apparent to Doug that his dad wasn't in top condition. "We don't have to go through with this," Doug offered. But Carl wanted to ride.

They got up early the next morning and took the charter bus out to Council Bluffs. The bus left them off in the official RAGBRAI site, a soccer complex off Interstate 80. The staging area was a zoo, Doug recalls, with massive traffic jams and people trying to get set for the next day's ride. There's always a great deal of confusion, uncertainty, and anxiety in the preride staging area. These sites are rarely pleasant, and, for newcomers to the ride, it can be overwhelming. The heat was oppressive, too. Doug and Carl cycled slowly out to the Missouri River to dip their back tires in the water—a RAGBRAI tradition. The rest of the afternoon Carl just sat on the ground, hanging his head. He was not a happy camper.

He finally got up and made the decision to bike into town, where they had arranged housing with a local family. They knew the roads would be busy, but they figured if they went slowly and rode carefully they could find their way safely. Soon they had to climb a bridge over the interstate. Doug was climbing slowly, but his dad called to him to back it down even more. Finally, Doug got off his bike to walk it on the sidewalk across the bridge. He was surprised when his dad cycled on past.

Then Doug watched, horrified, as his father wobbled in the busy traffic and flopped to the left, directly under the wheels of a pickup truck. There was nothing the driver could do. Doug says it was like time stopped and he was watching this scene unfold in slow motion. And then everything sped up. Doug was running back down the bridge to get police. Someone was doing CPR. A helicopter arrived to take Carl to the hospital, but he was pronounced dead on arrival. The truck tires had run over his torso. And Doug had witnessed the whole thing.

People back at the bike campsite rallied to take care of him. He was driven back to Grinnell. He remembers some minister had come along on the drive, and the man was helpful, but Doug had shut down. He was exhausted and dehydrated, utterly defeated. He was in therapy for many months after the experience.

As fate would have it, RAGBRAI was routed through Grinnell the very next year. Doug was shocked. He fired off an angry email to organizer Jim Green. But of course he realizes now that RAGBRAI is too big an organization to shift its route based on the emotional stability of one person. So Doug came to realize that he would have to confront the reality of the ride and what had happened. When Grinnell began to fill up with riders in 2001, Doug pedaled his bike around town and looked around. It wasn't so bad.

Since then, he has ridden at least a day of each succeeding ride, and did the entire ride in 2005 and 2006. "RAGBRAI is a wonderful thing," he affirms, "in spite of the terribly unfortunate circumstance that happened to me. RAGBRAI didn't kill my dad." He points out, with a chuckle, that one year he saw a RAGBRAI tee shirt for sale that read, "RAGBRAI killed Kenny," a twist on a line from the cartoon South Park. He was going to buy it, but it seemed in poor taste. The fact that he could laugh about it now is revealing. I relaxed with Doug at the overnight campsites this past year, sitting around the ice chests and swapping stories. "I had a blast," he said. His wife brought their two daughters out for a day and he pulled them for a few miles in a bike trailer—just the way I had started my kids on the ride. He says his mother doesn't get it yet—who can blame her? He doesn't tell her about riding each year until it's over.

Carl Cutchins was a special man who had touched many people through his professional and personal life. One of his former patients, acclaimed poet Mary Jo Salter, even wrote a poem in his honor.[47] His death on RAGBRAI was a blow that reverberated in pockets throughout the country. Every death has that effect.

Doug has one more twist to the story to tell. A childhood friend of his moved to Iowa. In 2001, the year after the death of Doug's father, she was diagnosed with renal failure. In January, 2002, Doug donated a kidney to her. He saw it as an opportunity to give back life. It was probably as therapeutic for him as it was life-saving for her. His friend is doing fantastic now. Inspired by Lance Armstrong, the professional cyclist who overcame cancer to win the Tour de France a record seven times, she picked up cycling. She competed in the U.S. Transplant Games in cycling events and came home with medals in 2004 and 2006. She participated in RAGBRAI in 2006, the year her role model, Lance, took part for a day. Doug says he saw Lance on the ride. Lance blew past him one day. Doug feels that things have come full circle.

Doug says, "I'm not to the point yet where I can say that my dad's death was a good thing. But positive things have come out of it." He is expressing a progressive Christian theology. He's not making the claim that God somehow caused this tragedy to happen for some unfathomable reason. He's just saying that there is grace that emerges. The day after the airliners were crashed into the World Trade Center and the Pentagon, Bill Moyers asked the Rev. James Forbes, senior pastor of the Riverside Church in Manhattan, where God was in this tragedy. Remember, many conservative Christian leaders were pointing the finger of blame already at gays and lifestyle choices, saying the terrorist attacks were God's just punishment for our nation's sins. Forbes had a different take. He said, in effect, "God didn't cause this tragedy. God was the first to shed a tear. God's heart was the first to break." And then God got busy and helped us come together as a nation to heal the wounds of people who were affected.

Doug is also echoing my sentiments from my previous book, *Blindsided by Grace: Entering the World of Disability*, in which I affirm that many good things have developed from my disabling accident. I was blindsided both by a hit-and-run driver in a pickup truck, and by many grace-filled blessings that have followed upon the injury. I'm not sure I ever would have chosen for this injury to happen, but now that it has, I have a choice either to complain about it or to go on with my life and find the value in it. In truth, the injury and how I have come to reflect on it have opened doors to me that never would have been opened otherwise.

Another wheelchair athlete who is from my home town often says "I had to break my neck to see the world." Her parents ran a convenience store in this town, and she probably would have gone into the family business. Following a car accident that left her in a wheelchair she moved to San Diego ("It was a winter day, ten below zero, when they released me from the hospital. I saw on the weather map that it was 80 in San Diego. So I moved there," she says) and got involved in the wheelchair athletics scene. She has now competed in over one hundred marathons all over the world.

One thing you often hear about sudden death is, "Well, at least he/she died doing what they loved." My own father died when I was just a junior in high school. We were at a barbershop music concert and he suffered a massive heart attack. I learned later that he had had a weak heart for decades; he had rheumatic fever in the 1940s. Doctors advised him not to marry or have children. But he led an active life and barbershop music was the love of his life. He died doing what he loved. In that, we're blessed. And so was he. He defied the odds, he lived to raise his sons at least into high school, and he was alive to the possibilities of life while he lived.

The question that bubbles to the surface, whether spoken or not, is, "If people can die while engaged in an exuberant, healthy, life-affirming activity like riding bikes, then when are we ever safe from death?" It's the same question we're asking in our "war on terrorism." If we're not safe in the heart of America, the strongest nation on the planet, especially now that we're spending billions of dollars on security measures, where can we be safe?

The answer to both questions is the same. We're never out from under the threat of mortality. Wear a helmet when you're cycling. That will help. Practice safe riding techniques. Take care of your health. But none of this changes the basic fact of mortality. We're never "safe." I think that's why our nation so overreacted to the attacks of 9/11, declaring preemptive war on a nation that had nothing to do with the attack. In my international experience I've found that many people around the world live with vulnerability all the time. They have accepted it as a fact of life. They have a hard time understanding why we were so shaken by an attack on our soil. Happens all around the world all the time.

Death is a part of living, woven into the fabric of creation from the very first. A theology that recognizes that bad things do indeed happen to good people is the healthiest one to live by. We're not going to cheat death through a healthy lifestyle or cosmetic surgery or medications or scientific breakthroughs or prayer. Or preemptive war or heightened security. The fact of death, like the war on terrorism, will never be overcome—and certainly not through exclusively military means. We may be able to postpone the inevitable for some months or years, but we can never change the basic fact. We live with the companionship of death as a constant. Our only option, then, is to decide how we are going to deal with that fact. Is it a tragedy to avoid until the last possible moment, or is it something we might want to "befriend," as Henri Nouwen puts it?

We go to extreme lengths in our society to avoid death and everything that reminds us of it, such as aging, illness, and disability. Most of the output of the Madison Avenue advertising machine is devoted to products designed to "protect" us against the onslaught of aging and dying. We buy anti-wrinkle cream, moisturizers, hair coloring, and fake tanning cream. There's that "little blue pill" for erectile dysfunction. There's liposuction and cosmetic surgery to make us look younger. There's the Thigh Master for her and the Hair Club for Men. There's taibo and the eight-minute abs workout. There's L'Oreal, because "you're worth it." Magazines are full of these ads, and people are spending billions of dollars on the products.

What's the obsession? Why can't we age as God intended? What's wrong with wrinkles and gray hair? And, ultimately, what's wrong with death? Other than the obvious fact that it cuts short a glorious bike ride, and, by extension, a viable life.

But death need not be an entirely unwanted companion. Henri Nouwen reflects on the spirituality of death in one of his books, *Our Greatest Gift: A Meditation on Dying and Death*. Leave it to Nouwen to find a way to talk about death as a gift. But he's right. Just as Michael J. Fox can claim that he is a "lucky man" to have been diagnosed with Parkinson's disease,[48] so Nouwen sees death as blessing. Bear with me here.

As he is engaged in ministry with many people who are facing death and families who have lost people they loved, Nouwen begins to question our aversion to the fact of death and our reluctance to even talk about it.

> Is death something so terrible and absurd that we are better off not thinking or talking about it? Is death such an undesirable part of our existence that we are better off

> acting as if it were not real? Is death such an absolute end of all our thoughts and actions that we simply cannot face it? Or is it possible to befriend our dying gradually and live open to it, trusting that we have nothing to fear? Is it possible to prepare for our death with the same attentiveness that our parents had in preparing for our birth? Can we wait for our death as for a friend who wants to welcome us home?[49]

Nouwen was startled when a friend asked him, "Where and how do you want to die?" It got him thinking. My wife and I led a very productive session with a high school youth group one time many years ago. We asked the young people to write their own obituaries. To do that, they would have to think about the reality of death and imagine how their lives might play out, and under what circumstances their lives might end. It was mostly an exercise about living, vocation, and imagination. But it also brought the reality of mortality in by the back door. I wrote mine. I wrote that I died a young man in a hail of gunfire, caught in crossfire between Latin American revolutionaries and U.S.-sponsored government troops. Don't ask me why. It was a whim. Like the question posed to Nouwen, this exercise got the students thinking and talking.

Nouwen wonders,

> Are we preparing ourselves for our death, or are we ignoring death by keeping busy? Are we helping each other to die, or do we simply assume we are going to always be here for each other? Will our death give new life, new hope, and new faith to our friends, or will it be no more than another cause for sadness?[50]

Sometimes the kindest, most enlightened thing to do at the bedside of a loved one at time of death is not to struggle heroically to prolong life, but to simply encourage the family to give the person permission to die. I've seen how patients hang on, struggling, trying to squeeze one more day or one more hour out of life, often for the sake of family members who they assume will be grief-stricken at their death. The one who is dying is trying to maintain control, to protect the feelings of those gathered by the bed, until the bitter end. When the reality of death can be openly acknowledged among all who have gathered, goodbyes said and permission given, the moments that follow can be holy and intimate.

Two weeks ago I was called out in the middle of the night by a distraught husband whose wife had been on a ventilator in a hospital intensive care room. He knew that his wife would not have wanted to remain like this, but her children and his—a blended family—were not all on the same page. In fact, it had been this woman's mission for the last nineteen years of her life to keep her "Brady Bunch" family together. She was the glue that bonded them. And now, at the time of her death, the ties were threatening to unravel. Finally, the medical people made it clear. The only thing keeping her alive was the ventilator. Her brain was gone. They were going to shut off the machines. The family had gathered, and they needed the presence of their pastor.

We gathered, a dozen or more of us, in a tiny room around this wife, mother, and grandmother, and said some prayers and read some scripture. I supported the family in its decision, and encouraged them to let her go. "Death comes into every life, whether welcome or not. Our one assurance is that, whether we live or whether we die, we belong to God. At this moment, as the machines are disconnected, we entrust this dear soul to God's care. We let her go. This is a holy moment. We are blessed to be here. Thanks be to God."

The ventilator was removed. The woman breathed on her own for a few hours longer, but before daybreak she had died. Her death, like her life, had pulled that family together and served as a sign of God's loving presence.

But how do we prepare to die on a bike ride? Or at any other time? How could I have prepared for my near-fatal accident that picture-perfect May afternoon in 1997? On that day I had been on a mission of celebration of the goodness of life. My day had consisted of an early morning run, bringing donuts home to my still-sleeping family, attending a high school graduation open house, a picnic lunch with my kids on the front porch of my house—Caitlin made tuna sandwiches by herself—sermon preparation out on the porch through the afternoon, and then that fateful bike ride I almost didn't return from. Who could have prepared for that? And why would anyone have wanted to?

Nouwen says, "When we know that God holds us safely—whatever happens—we don't have to fear anything or anyone but can walk through life with great confidence."[51] In other words, the best way to die well, and to be prepared for death whenever it may find us, is to live as fully as possible. Live like old Porter French did, or like my father did. As they say, live as though each day may be your last. Because it may.

> To befriend death, we must claim that we are children of God, sisters and brothers of all people, and parents of generations yet to come. In so doing, we liberate our death from its absurdity and make it the gateway to a new life.[52]

The threat of mortality is with us all the time. A bicycle ride across Iowa probably makes the incidence of death no more or less likely than any other experience we may have. It just makes death seem more removed somehow. Death is a natural stage in the process of living. God created us mortal, which implies from the get-go that one day we will not be here. I think that makes the experience of life more precious. I constantly remind people to live large and full, to extend one's life in love and to recognize and celebrate love where it is found. There is nothing more precious. William Sloane Coffin writes, "Without death, we'd never live. Without discovering the limits of our talents, we'd never discover who we are."[53] Love is the whole point of our religion, our scripture, our churches, and our bike rides across Iowa. Knowing that every relationship will eventually come to an end makes the love that much sweeter while it exists.

Coffin concludes:

> The more we do God's will, the less unfinished business we leave behind when we die. If our lives exemplify personal charity and the pursuit of social justice, then death will not be the enemy, but rather the friendly angel leading us on to the One whose highest hope is to be able to say to each and every one of us, "Well done, thou good and faithful servant; enter into the joy of the Master."[54]

Accepting the reality of death makes for more honest living. An honest life lived with integrity and passion for the task at hand and compassion for those around us is the highest ideal to which we can aspire.

I began this book with a quotation from Ecclesiastes to the effect that life is contradictory. "There is a time for every purpose under heaven." Life is not an orderly system, but a crucible for meaning into which inconsistencies and absurdities are thrown willy-nilly. We all stir the pot in our own way and pour out our personal concoction of meaning. Ecclesiastes may be disturbing to many, but the book is brutally honest.

It seems only fitting to close with another loose paraphrase of Ecclesiastes. The author is wondering about the point of all this toil and trouble. We put out all this effort in the project of life and what do we get to show for it? Nothing. Nada. Zippo. We can't take it with us. Every life will end, and at the end of our life, whatever we have built will get turned over to someone else. Most likely some idiot who won't appreciate what our accomplishments have meant. So what's the point?

He goes on to answer his rhetorical question, cynically, but honestly. "Since we're all going to die in the end and all is vanity anyway, there is nothing better for humans than to eat and drink, and ride RAGBRAI." That's not exactly what he said, but you get the idea. You've been given this life as a gift. It would be rude to leave it wrapped and untouched. Tear into the wrapping paper. Open it up. Try it on. Enjoy it. Wear it out. In the immortal words of the rock group, Queen, "Get on your bikes and ride!" I mean that literally. Go for a bike ride. Maybe I'll see you on the road and we'll make some meaning together.

EPILOGUE

The Lance Factor

LANCE ARMSTRONG participated in RAGBRAI for the first time in his career during the 2006 edition of the ride. Lance, in case you didn't know, rides his bike for a living. Or at least he did until his retirement from the sport in 2005. He claimed, when confronted about his absence from RAGBRAI in previous years, that he had been involved in some other bicycle ride during those weeks. Something called the Tour de France.

RAGBRAI participants have been inspired for years by the success of Armstrong, and, before him, Greg LeMond. LeMond and Armstrong catapulted American cycling to the forefront of international bicycle racing by winning the Tour de France, a three-week, two- to three-thousand mile bike race around Europe. LeMond has three Tour de France wins to his name. He was the first American to win this prestigious race. Armstrong has a record seven straight wins. RAGBRAI takes place during the last week of the Tour every year. We RAGBRAI riders used to get into town early and try to find a home or a church or a bar where we could flip on a TV and catch the results of the day's race. As Lance piled up seven wins of the world's most demanding bike race we all imagined ourselves to be as invincible as he seemed, charging hills and challenging head winds. Talk on the road frequently focused on the details of the day's Tour. How many seconds ahead was Lance (or Greg)? Who were his challengers? Would they be able to catch him in the mountains? Are they having as much fun as we are?

Then when Lance joined RAGBRAI for a day in 2006, offering two major speaking engagements, many of us were delirious with anticipation. Lance became the only show in town. "Where's Lance? Have you seen Lance? I rode with Lance for a few miles. I saw him breeze past me. I touched the hem of his shirt. He dripped sweat on me." It changed the complexion of the ride for that day.

Personally, I can't swear that he was ever actually on the ride. Like all the others, I was dying to see him. I actually carried a copy of my previous book that I was going to hand him on the road. (He was mentioned in that one, too. Lance seems to appear in all my books.) Never mind how I carried it. Never mind how he was going to carry it. I hoped he would notice me and ride a ways with me. I had things I wanted to tell him. Several times during the day I was close to him, apparently. Twice I came upon Lance-sightings. A crowd was gathered. People were talking about him. News crews were there interviewing people who claimed to have talked with him, ridden with him, touched him. But he wasn't there. For all I know he had been raptured. Or was he ever really there?

His presence also added an element of risk previously unknown on RAGBRAI. Lance doesn't ride at a leisurely pace. Given his history, I don't suppose he would know how. Lance's touring pace is several miles per hour faster than most strong riders' racing pace. So when Lance rides, he blows by most of the riders. But most of the riders also want to challenge The Man at his own game. I know I did. That had been my plan—to chase down the world's fastest cyclist on my handcycle. The Lance-a-lot Wannabees throw caution to the wind trying to catch his wheel and ride in his draft. So there were sections of highway last year with two hundred cyclists riding hell-bent at nearly thirty miles per hour, splintering the more leisurely flow of bicycle traffic on the road. There were several reports of accidents and crashes.

Lance has announced that he will ride every mile of RAGBRAI in 2007. As he put it, he's dipping his rear tire in the Missouri River and his front in the Mississippi. I'm sure I'm not the only bicyclist excited about having him along for the fun. Not only his cycling prowess, but his recovery from life-threatening cancer and return to the sport he loved, as well as his tireless advocacy for cancer research, have inspired me in my own recovery.

I hope Lance will read this book. To be sure, much of it he could have written himself. Who better than he knows about discipline and training? He's the world's foremost expert on short-term sacrifice for long-term goals. He won all those races because he was willing to endure more pain and suffering, both in training and in the race itself, than his competitors. I imagine he's also well-versed in issues of human mortality, especially as they relate to bicycling. A cancer survivor who was given far less than a 50-50 chance to beat the disease, he has stared death in the face. He's a team rider, so he understands teamwork and the role of community in contributing to his success. But I'm not sure he gets the fact that the point of life is in the journey, not the destination. Not yet, anyway. He's had to focus all these years on being the first to arrive in Paris. I doubt that he was enjoying the sunflowers along the route. If he approaches me on the RAGBRAI road and asks me for advice, I'll tell him that he needs to stop and smell the pork chops. Eat one or two each day. He should set himself an arbitrary speed limit one day—say, eight miles per hour if he can maintain his balance going that slowly—and assign himself a simple task, like stopping at every lemonade stand on the left side of the road. Or he could buy himself a knobby-tire Huffy for twenty bucks at a garage sale and join the ranks of the mere mortals on the ride. Perhaps wearing a kilt or a house dress or a loon on his helmet would help him see the ride from a different perspective. I could give him lots of pointers.

The participation of cycling's most prominent personality will change RAGBRAI, even if only for the week. The "ride-right" people, those who plan for the safety of the riders, are probably nervous about how to manage the crowds and dangerous riding tactics that Lance's presence, through no fault of his own, will engender. I know I would be. Lance is probably wondering how he's going to manage a week surrounded by the media frenzy he's sure to attract. The big story last year on the one day he rode was, "Lance Stops for a Beer! Film at 10:00." He stopped for a chat in a lady's front yard, someone produced a bottle of beer for him, he drank it, and it made the headlines. Just imagine a whole week of that. "Lance Takes a Cold Shower! Lance Spotted Sleeping! Lance Pees in a Cornfield!"

So we're all going to learn something on the 2007, thirty-fifth edition of the ride. RAGBRAI may be changed. Lance's presence may be good for the ride or bad for it. There are those who are saying that it may be the end of RAGBRAI as we know it. Of course, they've been predicting the demise of the ride every year since 1974 and they haven't been right yet. Lance may be changed. He may have an opportunity to experience a kind of playful, carefree, leisurely riding previously unknown to him—his first introduction to progressive Christian living. I hope so. RAGBRAI and Lance together might change the world. Maybe the publicity generated by Lance's presence will boost the sales of this book into bestseller categories, everyone will take my reflections seriously, and we'll find ourselves living in a kinder, gentler, more joyful world. Who knows? The Lance factor is just one more random element—an exciting random element—stirred into the pot. Meaning will emerge. It always does.

Endnotes

1. Rita Nakashima Brock, "Who Are These Progressive People of Faith?," *The Progressive Christian Witness: A Ministry of Pacific School of Religion* (www.progressivechristianwitness.org).

2. See Matthew Fox, *Original Blessing: A Primer in Creation Spirituality* (Santa Fe, NM: Bear and Company, 1983; New York: Jeremy P. Tarcher/Putnam, 2000).

3. John Karras and Ann Karras, *RAGBRAI: Everyone Pronounces It Wrong*. Ames: Iowa State University Press, 1999, p. 99.

4. Data from 2006 RAGBRAI Survey.

5. John Karras and Ann Karras, p. 78.

6. Ibid., p. 174.

7. RAGBRAI website: www.ragbrai.org

8. David Keirsey and Marilyn Bates, *Please Understand Me: Character and Temperament Types*. Del Mar, CA: Prometheus Nemesis Book Company, 1984, p. 22.

9. Karras and Karras, p. 48.

10. William Sloane Coffin, *Credo*. Louisville, KY: Westminster John Knox Press, 2004, p. 22

11. Ibid., p. 9.

12. Ibid., p. 53.

13. Marcus J. Borg, *Living the Questions*. Livingthequestions.com. 2004.

14. Jimmy Carter, *Our Endangered Values: America's Moral Crisis*. New York: Simon and Schuster, 2005, pp. 30-31.

15. Marcus J. Borg, *The Heart of Christianity: Rediscovering a Life of Faith*. New York: HarperCollins, 2003, p. 25.

16. John Shelby Spong, quoted in *Living the Questions*. See www.livingthequestions.com for more information.

17. Tex Sample, quoted in *Living the Questions*.

18. Spong, *Living the Questions*.

19. Robert Molsberry, *Blindsided by Grace: Entering the World of Disability*. Minneapolis, MN: Augsburg Fortress, 2004.

20. Henri J. M. Nouwen, *Here and Now: Living in the Spirit*. New York: Crossroad, 1997, p. 27.

21. Ibid., p. 29.

22. See Harold Kushner, *When Bad Things Happen to Good People*. HarperCollins, 1981.

23. Nouwen, p. 32.

24. Molsberry, p. vii.

25. Nouwen, pp. 17-19.

26. Matthew Fox, *On Becoming a Musical Mystical Bear: Spirituality American Style*. New York: Paulist Press, 1972, p. 29.

27. Karras and Karras, p. 45.

28. Ibid., p. 79.

29. Marcus J. Borg, *The God We Never Knew: Beyond Dogmatic Religion to a More Authentic Contemporory Faith*. San Francisco: HarperCollins 1997, p. 149.

30. Ibid., p. 145.

31. Coffin, p. 68.

32. *Living the Questions*, session 7.

33. Jim Wallace, *God's Politics: Why the Right Gets It Wrong and the Left Doesn't Get It*. New York: HarperCollins, 2005, p. xxii.

34. Ibid., pp. xxiii-xxiv.

35. Carter, pp. 178-179.

36. Coffin, p. 140.

37. Karras and Karras, p. 120.

38. Borg, *The God We Never Knew*, pp. 143-144.

39. Borg, p. 175.

40. Karras and Karras, p. 149.

41. M. Scott Peck, *The Road Less Traveled: A New Psychology of Love, Traditional Values and Spiritual Growth*. New York: Simon and Schuster, 1978, p. 15.

42. Ibid., pp. 15-16.

43. Richard J. Foster, *Celebration of Discipline*. New York: Harper & Row, 1978, p. 1.

44. Nouwen, *Here and Now*, p. 137.

45. Ibid., p. 91.

46. Ibid., p. 43.

47. See Mary Jo Salter's poem "Another Session," in *Open Shutters*, Knopf.

48. Michael J. Fox, *Lucky Man: A Memoir*. New York: Hyperion, 2002.

49. Henri J. M. Nouwen, *Our Greatest Gift: A Meditation on Dying and Death*. New York: HarperCollins, 1994, pp. xii-xiii.

50. Ibid., p. xvi.

51. Ibid., p. 16.

52. Ibid., p. 47.

53. Coffin, p. 167.

54. Ibid., p. 169.

About the Author

ROBERT MOLSBERRY, currently director of administration at Eden Theological Seminary in St. Louis, is an ordained United Church of Christ minister. A 1982 graduate of Yale Divinity School, he has served churches in Iowa and Illinois, and spent six years as a missionary in Central America directing community development.

Both before and after a 1997 hit-and-run accident that left him in a wheelchair, Molsberry has been active in athletics, competing in cycling and handcycing, wheelchair racing, swimming, and triathlon. His first book, *Blindsided by Grace: Entering the World of Disability* (2004) shares the story of his adjustment to his disability and his understanding of disability as a cross-cultural adventure.

Molsberry and his wife, Ann, who is also a United Church of Christ pastor, have two grown children who love RAGBRAI as much as he does. Ann, however, won't have a thing to do with the ride.